TRIO
READING 2

**The Intersection of
Vocabulary, Critical Thinking, & Reading**

Mari Vargo & Kate Adams

OXFORD

UNIVERSITY PRESS

OXFORD
UNIVERSITY PRESS

198 Madison Avenue
New York, NY 10016 USA

Great Clarendon Street, Oxford, OX2 6DP, United Kingdom

Oxford University Press is a department of the University of Oxford.
It furthers the University's objective of excellence in research, scholarship,
and education by publishing worldwide. Oxford is a registered trade
mark of Oxford University Press in the UK and in certain other countries

ISBN: 978 0 19 400403 9 STUDENT BOOK 2 WITH ONLINE PRACTICE PACK
ISBN: 978 0 19 400384 1 STUDENT BOOK 2 AS PACK COMPONENT
ISBN: 978 0 19 400387 2 ONLINE PRACTICE WEBSITE

Printed in China

This book is printed on paper from certified and well-managed sources

ACKNOWLEDGEMENTS

Cover Design: Yin Ling Wong

Illustrations by: Ben Hasler: Ben Hasler: 10, 11, 13, 15, 32, 33, 58, 62, 82, 109;
Joe Taylor: 20, 21, 44, 45, 70, 71, 74, 96, 120; 5W Infographics: 100, 115.

*The publishers would like to thank the following for their kind permission to reproduce
photographs:* JGI/Tom Grill/Getty Images, pg. 1 (violinist); Donald Bowers
Photography/Shutterstock, pg. 1 (long line); Anton_Ivanov/Shutterstock, pg.
1 (museum); JPagetRFPhotos/Shutterstock, pg. 7 (bathroom); SharkPaeCNX/
Shutterstock, pg. 7 (coffee); Prasit Rodphan/Shutterstock, pg. 7 (student
studying); ravipat/Shutterstock, pg. 7 (bicycle); Aleksander Bolbot/
Shutterstock, pg. 7 (forest); Chembarisov/Shutterstock, pg. 7 (ocean); vipman/
Shutterstock, pg. 7 (clothes); JGI/Tom Grill/Getty Images, pg. 7 (violinist);
Donald Bowers Photography/Shutterstock, pg. 7 (long line); Georgejmclittle/
Shutterstock, pg. 7 (phone); Deepak Budharaja/Getty Images, pg. 7 (family);
Anton_Ivanov/Shutterstock, pg. 7 (museum); Lorraine Swanson/Shutterstock,
pg. 9 (boys); Roberto Machado Noa/Contributor/Getty Images, pg. 9 (bus);
Henryk Sadura/Shutterstock, pg. 9 (skyscraper); Peter Dazeley/Getty Images,
pg. 9 (girl); JGI/Tom Grill/Getty Images, pg. 9 (violinist); JPagetRFPhotos/
Shutterstock, pg. 9 (bathroom); Georgejmclittle/Shutterstock, pg. 9 (phone);
Chembarisov/Shutterstock, pg. 9 (ocean); ravipat/Shutterstock, pg. 9 (bicycle);
SharkPaeCNX/Shutterstock, pg. 9 (coffee); Deepak Budharaja/Getty Images,
pg. 9 (family); Donald Bowers Photography/Shutterstock, pg. 9 (long line);
vipman/Shutterstock, pg. 9 (clothes); Aleksander Bolbot/Shutterstock, pg. 9
(forest); Prasit Rodphan/Shutterstock, pg. 9 (student studying); Anton_Ivanov/
Shutterstock, pg. 9 (museum); Luciano Mortula/Shutterstock, pg. 19 (Times
Square); Twin Design/Shutterstock, pg. 19 (kids on phones); Aspen Photo/
Shutterstock, pg. 19 (baseball player); testing/Shutterstock, pg. 45 (ping
pong); Robert Daly/Getty Images, pg. 45 (cleaning up trash); Portland
Press Herald/Contributor/Getty Images, pg. 45 (sports team); XiXinXing/
Shutterstock, pg. 45 (family at restaurant); Mike Powell/Getty Images, pg. 48
(goalie); Creative WO LatinContent/gilaimages/Getty Images, pg. 50 (sports
fans); digitalskillet/Getty Images, pg. 57 (women exercising); Three Lions/
Stringer/Getty Images, pg. 57 (baking bread); Charlesimage/Shutterstock,
pg. 57 (outdoor market); Chuck Savage/Corbis, pg. 59 (speaker); prudkov/
Shutterstock, pg. 59 (man on bench); Elena Elisseeva/Shutterstock, pg.
59 (exhausted girl); Photographee.eu/Shutterstock, pg. 59 (girl waving
at friends); Sorin Colac/Shutterstock, pg. 59 (Parthenon); Kunal Mehta/
Shutterstock, pg. 59 (modern building); wavebreakmedia/Shutterstock, pg.
64 (woman sleeping); SpeedKingz/Shutterstock, pg. 64 (man biking); Chicago
Tribune/Contributor/Getty Images, pg. 74 (macaroni and cheese); Lissandra
Melo/Shutterstock, pg. 74 (vending machine); imageBROKER/Alamy, pg. 76
(coal engine); Africa Studio/Shutterstock, pg. 77 (water wheel); Foodfolio/
the food passionates/Corbis, pg. 83 (washing dishes); Danny E Hooks/
Shutterstock, pg. 83 (soda in cooler); Steven Frame/Shutterstock, pg. 83 (man
holding money jar); Steven Errico/Getty Images, pg. 83 (man smelling milk);
Allen Donikowski/Getty Images, pg. 83 (ice cream cone); Tom Grill/Getty
Images, pg. 83 (flour and sugar canisters); Elena Elisseeva/Shutterstock/OUP,
pg. 85 (refrigerator); Corbis, pg. 86 (women carrying ice); Sergey Bogdanov/
Shutterstock, pg. 86 (stream); salajean/Shutterstock, pg. 86 (cave); Alexeysun/
Shutterstock, pg. 86 (sawdust); Grandpa/Shutterstock, pg. 86 (hole); Elena
Elisseeva/Shutterstock/OUP, pg. 86 (refrigerator); Alain Lauga/Shutterstock,
pg. 89 (thermopolium); Christian Kober/John Warburton-Lee Photography
Ltd/Getty Images, pg. 95 (Seoul); Monkey Business Images/Shutterstock,
pg. 95 (office); Mark Evans/Getty Images, pg. 95 (sports car); PaulPaladin/
Shutterstock, pg. 97 (different currencies); John Lund/Marc Romanelli/Getty
Images, pg. 97 (discussing artwork); MR.LIGHTMAN1975/Shutterstock, pg.
97 (financial diagram); Happyture/Shutterstock, pg. 97 (people walking to
work); IllyaBel/Shutterstock, pg. 102 (Paris); MARWAN NAAMANI/Staff/Getty
Images, pg. 102 (Dubai); Yolanta/Shutterstock, pg. 103 (London); Monkey
Business Images/Shutterstock, pg. 108 (kids playing); Brian A Jackson/
Shutterstock, pg. 108 (visitor pass); Picsfive/Shutterstock, pg. 108 (math
problems); terekhov igor/Shutterstock, pg. 108 (office interior); ColorBlind
Images/Getty Images, pg. 108 (students in library); Nitr/Shutterstock, pg. 108
(coffee and tea); Floresco Productions/Corbis, pg. 112 (workers in cubicles);
Monty Rakusen/Getty Images, pg. 112 (chocolate factory); Steve Dunwell/
Getty Images, pg. 112 (robot); g-stockstudio/Shutterstock, pg. 119 (fun office
environment); dizain/Shutterstock, pg. 121 (flowchart); Blend Images/Blend
Images/SuperStock, pg. 121 (girl recycling); Bogdan Mihai Romeo/Alamy, pg.
121 (car exhaust); Garo/Phanie/SuperStock, pg. 121 (food coloring); smereka/
Shutterstock, pg. 124 (wood); BanksPhotos/Getty Images, pg. 124 (concrete);
Instinia/Shutterstock, pg. 124 (steel); Tony Watson/Alamy, pg. 124 (glue);
SiliconValleyStock/Alamy, pg. 127 (traffic).

REVIEWERS

We would like to acknowledge the following individuals for their input during the development of the series:

Mahmoud Al-Salah
University of Dammam
Saudi Arabia

Robert J. Ashcroft
Tokai University
Japan

Karen E. Caldwell
Bahrain Polytechnic
Bahrain

Stephanie da Costa Mello
Glendale Community College
U.S.A.

Travis Cote
Tamagawa University
Japan

Ian Daniels
Smart ELT
Japan

Gail Fernandez
Bergen Community College
U.S.A.

Theresa Garcia de Quevedo
Geos Boston English Language School
U.S.A.

Patricia Ishill
Union County College
U.S.A.

Ji Hoon Kim
Independence English Institute
South Korea

Masakazu Kimura
Katoh Gakuen Gyoshu High School/
Nihon University
Japan

Georgios-Vlasios Kormpas
Al Yamamah University/SILC
Saudi Arabia

Ji-seon Lee
Jeong English Campus
South Korea

Sang-lee Lee
Kangleong Community Language
Center
South Korea

Zee Eun Lim
Reader's Mate
South Korea

James MacDonald
Aspire Language Academy
Kaohsiung City

Chaker Ali Mhamdi
Al Buraimi University College
Oman

Elizabeth R. Neblett
Union County College
U.S.A.

John Peloghitis
Tokai University
Japan

Whitney Tullos
Intrax
U.S.A.

Pingtang Yen
Eden Institute
Taichung City

Author Acknowledgments

I'd like to thank my family for their support, Jennifer Wilson Cooper for introducing me to the world of content development, and Crockett for being my partner in crime.

—Mari Vargo

A special thanks to my mentor in Teaching English as a Second Language at Northeastern Illinois University, Dr. Teddy Bofman, who counseled me that education is never over. A thank you to my students at the Illinois Institute of Technology for sharing their opinions, thoughts, and pursuits with me and to the community of faculty and friends I've met along the way.

Many thanks to Eliza Jensen for her discerning eye and diligent work on *Trio Reading* and to Anna Norris for sharing her enthusiasm and opinions in developing this series. Both were valuable collaborators.

And a thank you to my husband and son, my lifelong learning partners.

—Kate Adams

CONTENTS

Welcome to Trio Reading

Building Better Readers . . . From the Beginning

Trio Reading includes three levels of Student Books, Online Practice, and Teacher Support.

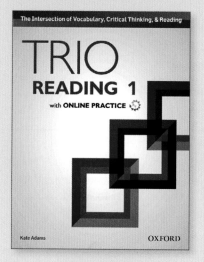

Level 1/CEFR A1

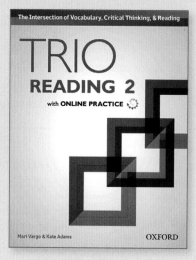

Level 2/CEFR A2

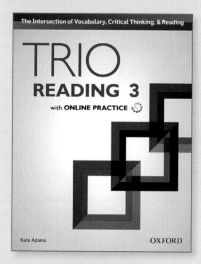

Level 3/CEFR B1

Essential Digital Content

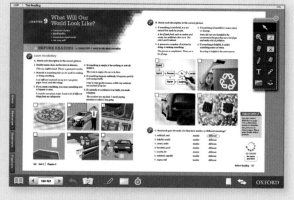

iTools USB with Classroom Resources

Trio Reading's contextualized vocabulary instruction, accessible paired readings, and critical thinking activities provide students with the tools they need for successful academic reading at the earliest stages of language acquisition.

Vocabulary Based On the Oxford 2000 ✏ Keywords

Trio Reading's vocabulary is based on the 2,000 most important and useful words to learn at the early stages of language learning, making content approachable for low-level learners.

Making Connections for Critical Thinking

Make Connections sections encourage the development of critical thinking skills by asking learners to draw connections between themselves, texts, and the world around them.

Readiness Unit

For added flexibility, each level of *Trio Reading* begins with an optional Readiness Unit to provide fundamental English tools for beginning students.

INSIDE EACH CHAPTER

BEFORE READING

Theme-based chapters set a context for learning.

Essential, explicit skills help beginning learners to gain confidence with academic reading texts.

CHAPTER 4 **Has Exercise Always Been Important?**

- Past tense /d/, /t/, and /ɪd/ sounds
- Descriptive adjectives
- Identify cause and effect
- Irregular past tense verbs

BEFORE READING ▸ Oxford 2000 words to talk about exercise

Learn Vocabulary

A. Match each picture to the correct description.

____ A **cause** makes something happen.
The cause of the fire was a candle.

__1__ An **effect** is the result of something.
Eating well is having a positive effect on my health.

____ If someone is **fit**, he or she is healthy.
Erica exercises a lot. She's really fit.

____ **Evidence** is proof or shows that something is true.
We found evidence that there was a house here in the past.

1. 
2. 
3. 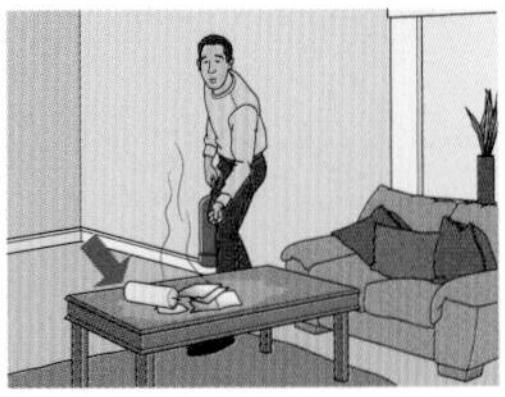
4. 

58 Unit 2 | Chapter 4

B. Look at each picture. Complete each sentence with a word from the box.

calm	~~nervous~~	include	ancient	energy	modern

1. 
When you are __nervous__, you are worried. You don't feel relaxed.

2. 
When you are ________, you feel relaxed.

3. 
When you don't have a lot of ________, you feel tired and you don't want to do anything.

4. 
If you ________ someone, you invite that person to join you.

5. 
If something is ________, it is extremely old.

6. 
If something is ________, it is of the present or recent times.

C. Complete the paragraph with the words from the box. You won't use two of the words.

calm	~~cause~~	effects	energy	fit	modern	nervous

Do you feel tired in the afternoon? Many different things can __cause__ sleepiness during the day. A big lunch, a sugary snack, or sitting for a long time can make you tired. When you feel tired in the afternoon, don't drink coffee. It's true that coffee can have positive ________. For example, it can give you ________. However, too much coffee can make you feel ________. Instead, take a walk. That way, you can wake up and get ________ at the same time.

Oxford 2000
Use the Oxford 2000 list on page 133 to find more words to describe the pictures on these pages. Share your words with a partner.

GO ONLINE for more practice

Before Reading | 59

Vocabulary is introduced in context and is built from the Oxford 2000 list of keywords.

Trio Reading Online Practice extends learning beyond the classroom, providing students with additional practice and support for each chapter's vocabulary, grammar, and skills instruction.

Sounds of English

Spelling Connection

A. There are three possible ending sounds for regular past tense verbs: /d/, /t/, and /ɪd/. We say the /d/ sound after the voiced sounds like /b/, /g/, /v/, /z/, /m/, /n/, /l/, and all vowels. We say the /t/ sound after the voiceless sounds like /p/, /k/, /s/, and /f/. We say the /ɪd/ sound after /t/ and /d/ sounds. Listen to the examples.

/d/	/t/	/ɪd/
played	*liked*	*wanted*
called	*missed*	*decided*

B. Listen to the simple past verbs. Circle the ending sound that you hear.

1. worked	a. /d/	b. /t/ (circled)	c. /ɪd/
2. invented	a. /d/	b. /t/	c. /ɪd/
3. used	a. /d/	b. /t/	c. /ɪd/
4. started	a. /d/	b. /t/	c. /ɪd/
5. cared	a. /d/	b. /t/	c. /ɪd/

Sounds of English boxes provide sound-symbol decoding practice and link fluency and reading skills to improve students' reading speed and comprehension.

▲▲ DURING READING

Accessible paired readings help students develop reading skills by offering more reading practice and the opportunity to make connections between texts.

Vocabulary Strategies and Reading Strategies are practiced with each reading, giving students the skills they need for successful reading.

Audio for each reading helps students make the link between spoken and written English.

Grammar in the Readings boxes highlight the most important language from the readings. Practice of each grammar point is provided as part of *Trio Reading* Online Practice.

▲▲ DURING READING
► Vocabulary strategy: Descriptive adjectives
► Reading strategy: Identify cause and effect

◉ Reading 1

A. Read the text. If you don't understand something, look back and ahead a few words to see if that makes the meaning clearer.

Did People in the Past Exercise?

Exercise is a part of many people's lives today. Many people swim, work out at gyms, or play sports several times a week because they want to be physically **fit**. But **modern** people didn't invent exercise. Was exercise popular in the past? The answer is yes! Exercise for physical fitness wasn't as popular in the past as it is today. However, people have been interested in exercise for thousands of years.

No one knows exactly when humans began to exercise, but we do know that exercise was very important in certain **ancient** civilizations. In ancient China, people knew that physical activity could help them stay healthy. So sometime between the 17th century BCE and 250 BCE, kung fu was invented in China. Today, people practice kung fu all over the world.

Yoga is another ancient exercise. It is also common today. Yoga was invented in India. It involves stretching, movement, and breathing exercises. There is **evidence** that people were practicing yoga at least 5,000 years ago. Ancient stones from 3000 BCE **include** carvings of people in yoga poses. However, many people believe that yoga didn't start in 3000 BCE. They think it began much earlier than that.

Exercise [...] important in [...] Greeks prob[...]

than any other group of people. They thought that exercising the body was as important as exercising the mind. Therefore, they made exercise a big part of their society. Some of the types of exercise that the Greeks enjoyed included gymnastics, running, jumping, and wrestling—a type of fighting. The ancient Greeks created the Olympic Games in 776 BCE. For almost 12 centuries, athletes competed in the Games every four years. Today, countries all over the globe compete in the Olympic Games.

Physical fitness has been a part of human history for thousands of years. Exercises and events that began far in the past continue today. Do you think that exercises and events from

Stop and Think
Why do you think no one really knows when people started exercising?

62   Unit 2 | Chapter 4

Check Your Understanding

B. Write three examples of exercise in the past.
1. _____
2. _____
3. _____

Vocabulary Strategy

Descriptive Adjectives
Descriptive adjectives give more information about nouns. They usually describe things like feelings, taste, appearance, size, color, and shape. Learning descriptive adjectives will help you understand the details the writer includes. Look at the examples.

*Sarah is **nervous**.*   *I feel **calm**.*   *The soup is **hot**.*

C. Read each set of words. Circle the word that is NOT a descriptive adjective.

1. exciting	example	convenient	social
2. rude	enjoyable	successful	game
3. exercise	healthy	interesting	happy
4. sad	large	round	enjoy
5. modern	play	great	angry

D. Look at the words you circled in Activity C. What part of speech is each word? Write the word and the part of speech.

1. example / noun   2. _____
3. _____   4. _____
5. _____

Reading Strategy

Identify Cause and Effect
A *cause* is the reason that something happened. An *effect* is the thing that happened. Writers use certain words to describe cause and effect relationships. Understanding these words will help you identify the causes and effects when you read. Here are some examples.

to describe a cause: *because*   *because of*

GO ONLINE for more practice

E. Look at the text on page 62. Find and underline an example of each word or phrase. Then write the cause and effect.

1. because   cause: _____
              effect: _____
2. so   cause: _____
        effect: _____
3. therefore   cause: _____
               effect: _____

◉ Reading 2

A. Listen and read along.

What Are the Effects of Exercise?

You probably already know that exercise can help you lose weight and stay fit. However, it has a lot of other good **effects**, too. Are you healthy and fit? Even if you are, there are several reasons that you should exercise.

First, exercise can give you **energy**. When you are tired during the day and you can't study or work, don't take a nap. Take a walk or go for a run instead. Researchers looked at 70 different studies about exercise and fatigue— extreme tiredness. In the studies, people who didn't exercise started to exercise

regularly. As a result, they felt less fatigue. They didn't feel tired during the day. Over 90 percent of the studies showed the same results: regular exercise increased energy and reduced fatigue.

Second, exercise can help you sleep better. It's important to get enough sleep. Lack of sleep is one of the main **causes** of stress. Exercising raises your body temperature. Your temperature goes back to normal about five to six hours after you exercise. You become sleepy at this point because the drop in temperature tells your body that it's time to sleep.

Also, exercise can reduce stress and anxiety. Do you ever feel **nervous** or

stressed? Working out for 20 minutes can make you feel **calm**. How? When you exercise, you have to focus on your body, so you can't think about your stressful thoughts. In addition, when you exercise, your body creates a special chemical. This chemical can help your brain react to stress.

Finally, studies show that exercise is good for your brain, especially your memory. Exercising makes your body

create new cells in a part of the brain called the hippocampus. Memory and learning happen in the hippocampus. Because of this increase in cells, exercising can improve your memory and make it easier to learn new things.

Regular exercise can improve your life in so many ways. It can make you feel better, look better, and do more. So why are you sitting there reading? Go out and exercise!

Stop and Think
What do you do when you feel tired during the day? Do you think this is the best thing to do?

Grammar in the Readings

Notice irregular past tense verbs in the readings.

Some verbs are irregular in the simple past tense. You have to memorize these forms.

begin → began   go → went   feel → felt
make → made   take → took   think → thought

*People **began** exercising thousands of years ago.*
*They **thought** exercise was important.*

Irregular past tense verbs stay the same for all subjects.

*I **took** a nap.*   *She **took** a nap.*   *They **took** naps.*

Check Your Understanding

B. Write four effects of exercise.

Effect 1	Effect 2

Effects of Exercise

Effect 3	Effect 4

GO ONLINE for grammar practice

64   Unit 2 | Chapter 4

During Reading   65

viii

▲▲▲ AFTER READING

Summarizing and Retelling activities provide students with the opportunity to review the concepts and vocabulary learned throughout the chapter.

Three Make Connections sections in each chapter help students develop critical thinking skills by linking texts to their own lives, other texts, and the wider world.

▲▲▲ AFTER READING

Summarizing and Retelling

A. Complete the sentences with the words from the box. Then read the sentences to a partner to summarize.

Nouns	Verbs	Adjectives
cause	include	ancient
effects		calm
energy		fit
evidence		modern
		nervous

1. There is _____ that people have been exercising for thousands of years.
2. For example, a(n) _____ stone tablet from 3000 BCE shows people doing yoga.
3. Types of sports _____ swimming, soccer, and golf.
4. Kung fu is an old sport that is still popular in _____ times.
5. Exercising has a lot of good _____.
6. First, it makes us healthy and _____.
7. If we're stressed or _____, exercising for 20 minutes can make us feel _____.
8. Not getting enough sleep can be a(n) _____ of stress. Exercise can reduce stress.
9. If you feel tired, exercise can give you more _____.

B. Answer the questions with a partner.

1. There is evidence that people started exercising thousands of years ago. Think about the country you live in. Do you think people there two hundred years ago exercised as much as people today? Why or why not?
2. What do you think is the most important effect of exercise for you? Explain.

Word Partners

take a nap
take a walk
take medicine
take a break
take some time off

GO ONLINE to practice word partners

◖◗ Make Connections: Text to World

A. Answer the questions.

1. Do you think people today exercise enough? Too much? Explain.
_____
_____

2. Imagine that it is the year 4000. What kinds of evidence do you think people will find that show that we used to exercise?
_____
_____

3. What are some reasons that companies should give employees time to exercise during the day? Explain.
_____
_____
_____

4. What are some other ways to:
reduce stress and anxiety?
_____
_____

increase your energy?
_____
_____

improve your sleep?
_____
_____

improve your memory?
_____
_____

B. Talk about your answers from Activity A with a partner. Look at the Oxford 2000 keywords on page 133 and find five words to help you.

Chant

GO ONLINE for the Chapter 4 Vocabulary & Grammar Chant

Word Partners activities expand on vocabulary taught in the chapter so students acquire more high-frequency collocations.

Vocabulary and Grammar Chants found online help students internalize the target grammar structure and vocabulary for greater fluency when reading.

Trio Reading Online Practice: Essential Digital Content

Trio Reading Online Practice provides multiple opportunities for skills practice and acquisition—beyond the classroom and beyond the page.

Each unit of *Trio Reading* is accompanied by a variety of automatically graded activities. Students' progress is recorded, tracked, and fed back to the instructor.

Vocabulary and Grammar Chants help students internalize the target grammar structure and vocabulary for greater accuracy and fluency when reading.

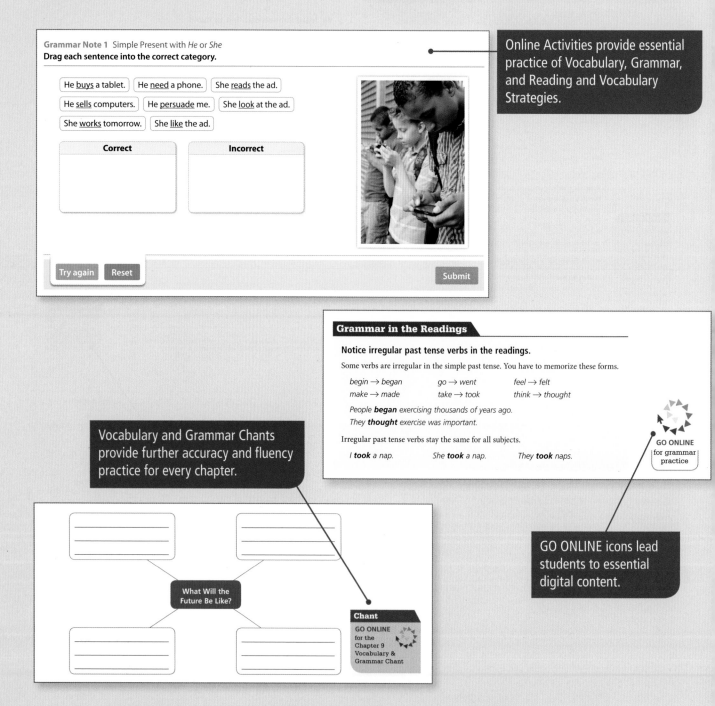

Grammar Note 1 Simple Present with *He* or *She*
Drag each sentence into the correct category.

He <u>buys</u> a tablet.　He <u>need</u> a phone.　She <u>reads</u> the ad.

He <u>sells</u> computers.　He <u>persuade</u> me.　She <u>look</u> at the ad.

She <u>works</u> tomorrow.　She <u>like</u> the ad.

Correct	**Incorrect**

Try again　Reset　Submit

Online Activities provide essential practice of Vocabulary, Grammar, and Reading and Vocabulary Strategies.

Grammar in the Readings

Notice irregular past tense verbs in the readings.

Some verbs are irregular in the simple past tense. You have to memorize these forms.

begin → began　　*go → went*　　*feel → felt*
make → made　　*take → took*　　*think → thought*

*People **began** exercising thousands of years ago.*
*They **thought** exercise was important.*

Irregular past tense verbs stay the same for all subjects.

*I **took** a nap.*　　*She **took** a nap.*　　*They **took** naps.*

GO ONLINE for grammar practice

GO ONLINE icons lead students to essential digital content.

Vocabulary and Grammar Chants provide further accuracy and fluency practice for every chapter.

What Will the Future Be Like?

Chant
GO ONLINE for the Chapter 9 Vocabulary & Grammar Chant

Use the access code on the inside front cover to log in at **www.oxfordlearn.com/login**.

Readiness Unit

Words

Letters and sounds
Word patterns
Syllables
Stressed and unstressed syllables

Parts of Speech

Nouns
Adjectives
Verbs
Verb tenses

Sentences and Paragraphs

Sentences
Questions
Paragraphs
⬤ Make connections

UNIT WRAP UP Extend Your Skills

▲ WORDS

Letters and sounds

The English alphabet has 26 letters. Say the names of the letters of the alphabet:

a b c d e f g h i j k l m n o p q r s t u v w x y z

These letters are vowels:

a e i o u

Sometimes they make the sound of their letter name. Other times they make a different sound.

A. Look at the sounds. Write each word from the box in the correct column.

ask	day	last	~~pattern~~	they
bad	family	make	~~pay~~	train

short a /æ/	long a /eɪ/
pattern	pay

B. Look at the sounds. Write each word from the box in the correct column.

be	cheat	egg	feature	~~see~~
bed	desk	feather	meet	~~set~~

short e /ɛ/	long e /i/
set	see

C. Look at the sounds. Write each word from the box in the correct column.

find	limit	pie	~~skill~~	thin
item	my	risk	system	~~write~~

short i /ɪ/	long i /aɪ/
skill	write

D. Look at the sounds. Write each word from the box in the correct column.

along	boat	complicate	explode	~~hot~~
arrow	both	doctor	~~go~~	lock

short o /ɑ/	long o /oʊ/
hot	go

E. Look at the sounds. Write each word from the box in the correct column.

~~but~~	love	new	too	unfair
~~blue~~	lunch	study	true	

short u /ʌ/	long u /u/
but	blue

F. There are other vowel sounds. Look at the sounds below. Match each word to another word with the same sound.

1. /ʊ/ put _____c_____   a. voice

2. /ɔɪ/ boy _____   b. how

3. /aʊ/ now _____   c. foot

G. The schwa sound /ə/ in _about_ can be spelled with any vowel. Circle the vowel in each word that makes the schwa sound.

1. ben(e)fit   2. along   3. profit   4. pilot   5. supply

H. These vowel sounds have an /r/ sound with them. Say each word and listen to the sound.

1. /ər/ bird   2. /ɑr/ car   3. /ɛr/ hair

4. /ɪr/ near   5. /ʊr/ tour   6. /ɔr/ north

Word patterns

Some words have the same pattern of letters. The spelling is the same. They rhyme. The ending sounds are the same.

    cake   take   make   lake

A. Cross out the word in each row that does NOT rhyme.

1. map   lap   ~~lip~~   sap   tap

2. cop   mop   top   nap   stop

3. stay   bay   away   jay   rays

4. wood   fold   stood   hood   good

Some words rhyme, but they have different letters. The spelling patterns are different.

    chair/bear

B. Match each word to the word that rhymes.

1. moon _____e_____   a. crowd

2. neat _____   b. late

3. loud _____   c. sheet

4. made _____   d. laid

5. eight _____   e. tune

Syllables

Words are made of syllables. Each syllable has a vowel sound. Say each syllable in the words below.

read	book•shelf	com•pre•hend
1	1 2	1 2 3

> The letter *y* can sound like a vowel.
>
> The letter *y* sounds like a long i /aɪ/ in a one-syllable word.
>
> *fly   my   cry*
>
> It sounds like a long e /i/ when a consonant is before it and it ends a two-syllable word.
>
> *ba•by*

A. Cross out the word in each row that has a different number of syllables.

1. be   late   it   ~~lady~~

2. idea   sun   picture   punish

3. project   work   get   make

4. nothing   mother   operate   improve

5. general   difficult   manage   terrible

B. Write the number of syllables in each word.

1. many   be   before   transportation
   2 ___   ___   ___   ___

2. write   himself   look   syllable
   ___   ___   ___   ___

3. sense   language   textbook   world
   ___   ___   ___   ___

4. shape   success   understanding anyone
   ___   ___   ___   ___

5. return   computer   send   messages
   ___   ___   ___   ___

Stressed and unstressed syllables

In words with more than one syllable, one syllable is stressed. You say the vowel sound in the stressed syllable for a little longer than the other vowels.

A. Read each word. Stress the correct syllable.

1. PA•per   2. a•CROSS   3. com•PU•ter   4. LA•ter   5. re•FLECT   6. BA•by

B. The schwa /ə/ sound is not stressed. Read each word with the schwa. Stress the other syllable. Say the vowel sound in that word longer.

1. a•BOUT   2. a•LONG   3. TAR•get

C. Underline the stressed syllable in each word.

1. <u>mir</u>|ror   2. con|duct   3. sal|ad

4. fin|ger   5. own|er   6. cov|er

D. Draw a line to show the syllables in each word. Then underline the stressed syllable.

1. sug|<u>gest</u>   2. statement   3. sentence   4. partner   5. discuss

E. Match each word to the word with the same number of syllables and the same stressed syllable.

1. ability   ___d___   a. language

2. poor   _____   b. prefer

3. money   _____   c. more

4. frequency _____   d. analysis

5. before   _____   e. celebrate

PARTS OF SPEECH

Nouns

Some words are nouns. These words name people, places, and things.

A. Look at each picture. Fill in the missing letters to spell each noun from the box.

bathroom	clothes	crowd	female	museum	ocean
bicycle	coffee	family	forest	musician	phone

1. b _a_ _t_ hro _o_ m

2. co ___ fe ___

3. ___ em ___ le

4. b ___ c ___ c ___ e

5. ___ or ___ st

6. ___ ce ___ n

7. c ___ o ___ he ___

8. m ___ sic ___ a ___

9. c ___ o ___ d

10. ___ ho ___ e

11. ___ ami ___ ___

12. m ___ s ___ um

B. Which nouns are people, which are places, and which are things? Write each noun from the box in the correct column.

bathroom	clothes	crowd	female	museum	ocean
bicycle	coffee	family	forest	~~musician~~	phone

People	Places	Things
musician		

Some nouns name ideas or feelings. We call them *abstract nouns* because you can't see them. Many abstract nouns have common word endings. These word endings are called *suffixes*. You can identify which words are nouns by identifying their suffixes. Look at the suffixes on the nouns below.

measure**ment**   educa**tion**   happi**ness**

C. Which words are nouns? Look for suffixes. Circle the nouns in each row. There is more than one noun in each row.

1. (appointment)	inform	make	now	(collection)
2. announcement	get	illness	analyze	back
3. development	kindness	purple	almost	take
4. sadness	angry	situation	solution	concentrate
5. tradition	complete	write	friendly	information

There are two kinds of nouns in English, count and noncount nouns. Count nouns are things you can count. You can tell how many there are. Noncount nouns are for things you can't count.

D. Circle the nouns in each sentence. Then write each noun in the correct column.

1. My brother likes to climb trees.

2. I like sugar in my tea.

3. I bought some milk at the store.

4. My friends talk on the phone all day.

Count Nouns	Noncount Nouns
brother	sugar

Adjectives

Some words are adjectives. They describe nouns. Adjectives can be numbers, colors, and describing words to tell about size, feelings, or other characteristics.

number: *three boys*

color: *yellow bus*

size: *tall skyscraper*

feelings: *upset girl*

A. Look at each picture. Write a phrase to describe it with an adjective from the box. You will not use all of the words.

| beautiful | blue | dark | happy | interesting | new | ~~serious~~ |
| big | clean | dirty | hot | old | red | smart |

1. *serious musician*

2. _____

3. _____

4. _____

5. _____

6. _____

7. _____

8. _____

9. _____

10. _____

11. _____

12. _____

B. Look at each picture. Write an adjective to tell about the noun.

1. feelings: _____happy_____ boy

2. size: _____ package

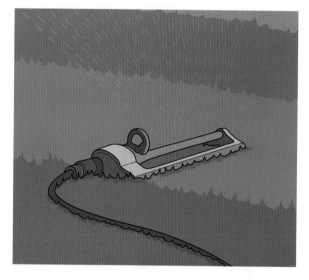

3. color: _____ grass

4. number: _____ women

You can also identify adjectives from their suffixes. Adjectives often use the suffixes *-ous*, *-tive*, and *-able*. Look at the suffixes on the adjectives below.

fam**ous**   nega**tive**   enjoy**able**

C. Which words are adjectives? Look for suffixes. Circle the adjectives in each row. There is more than one adjective in each row.

1. (reasonable)	map	(positive)	manager	work
2. do	various	dangerous	baby	walked
3. expensive	excitement	speak	comfortable	gave
4. experiment	nervous	exclamation	serious	made
5. attractive	attraction	read	improvement	available

Verbs

Some words are verbs. Some verbs show action. They tell what nouns do. Other verbs tell what nouns are. We call these verbs *linking verbs* because they link a noun to another noun or adjective.

A. Look at each picture. Fill in the missing letters to spell each verb from the box.

dream	examine	go	look	meet	think
enter	~~give~~	laugh	make	tell	work

1. _g_ i _v_ e

2. t __ in __

3. te __ __

4. m __ __ e

5. __ o __ k

6. __ oo __

7. __ o

8. e __ t __ r

9. e __ am __ __ e

10. l __ __ gh

11. d __ __ am

12. m __ e __

B. Circle the verb in each sentence. Then write it in the correct column.

1. My mother is a nurse.

2. We are students.

3. I meet lots of people.

4. I work in an office.

5. I go home after work.

6. The doctor examines children when they are sick.

7. I laugh a lot.

8. My dad makes movies.

9. I am a teacher.

10. We are friends.

Action Verbs (Tell What Nouns Do)	Linking Verbs (Tell What Nouns Are)
meet	is

Verb tenses

The *tense* of a verb shows when something happened.

We use present tense for things that happen now. Add *-s* to verbs in the present tense when the subject is singular.

work + -s = works   *She works.*

We use past tense for things that happened before, in the past.

Some verbs are regular. Add *-ed* to regular verbs to form the past tense.

look + -ed = looked

Other verbs are irregular. The past tense form is different from the present tense.

run = ran

A. Circle the verb in each sentence.

Present Tense

1. Today, I look out the window.

3. Today, I run around the track.

5. I give the teacher my homework.

7. He makes plans.

9. I work in Tokyo.

Past Tense

2. Yesterday, I looked out the window.

4. Yesterday, I ran around the track.

6. I gave the teacher my homework.

8. He made plans.

10. I worked in Tokyo.

B. Write each verb from Activity A in the correct column.

Regular Verbs	Irregular Verbs
look / looked	run / ran

SENTENCES AND PARAGRAPHS

Sentences

A sentence tells an idea. We use words to write sentences.

I have a question.

A sentence begins with a capital letter and ends with a period.

We enjoy studying.

capital letter ⬆   period ⬆

A. Match each picture to the correct sentence.

_____ The children play at the park.   _____ The manager talks to his employees.

__1__ The woman enjoys nature.   _____ I can relax on an airplane.

B. Write a sentence for each picture below. Use a capital letter and period.

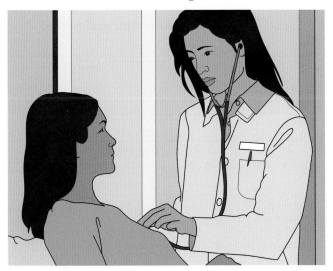 

_____   _____

_____   _____

Questions

A sentence can ask a question. A question ends with a question mark and needs an answer.

Some questions have *yes* or *no* answers.

Question: *Do you like to study?*

↑
question mark

Answer: *Yes, I like to study.*

Some questions ask for information.

Question: *Where are you from?*
Answer: *I am from India.*

A. Look at the different question word that begins each sentence. Match each question to its answer.

1. **What** do you study? __b__

2. **When** do you go to bed? _____

3. **How** are you? _____

4. **Who** do you know here? _____

5. **Why** are you driving? _____

6. **Where** are you going? _____

a. I'm walking to the bank.

b. ~~I'm taking an English class.~~

c. I am Cecilia's friend.

d. I don't want to walk.

e. I am OK.

f. I go to sleep around 11 o'clock.

Paragraphs

We use sentences to create paragraphs. The sentences in the paragraph talk about the same thing.

A. Reorder each set of words to make a sentence. Use a capital letter and period.

1. make / sentences / words _Words make sentences._

2. a / paragraph / called / is / of / group / a / sentences _____

_____

3. words / letters / make _____

4. a main / paragraphs / idea / have / details / and _____

_____

5. communicate / to / we / sentences / use _____

_____

B. Read the title. Then reorder the sentences from Activity A to make a paragraph.

How We Communicate

_____

_____

_____

_____

_____

C. Look at the picture. Read the paragraph. Circle the correct answer.

Many people like to read. What do you read? Do you like to read the newspaper, magazines, books, or textbooks? These texts have different types of writing. Textbooks teach a school subject. Books often tell stories, and magazines and newspapers share current information or stories. Do you read for school or do you read for pleasure? When you read for pleasure, you read what you like. You enjoy what you read.

1. What can you learn from the picture?

   a. what pleasure is   b. things people read   c. things people read at school

2. What is *pleasure*?

   a. doing something for school   b. reading   c. enjoying something

3. According to the paragraph, what text often tells stories?

   a. textbooks   b. information   c. books

4. What is the topic of the paragraph?

   a. texts people read   b. information people learn   c. textbooks teach

D. Match each text to the correct title.

_____ Pronunciation and the Sounds of Language

_____ Why Is Word Order Important?

_____ What Is a Complete Sentence?

1.　　Languages use sentences. The words in the sentence are in a specific order. For example, in English the order is subject, verb, object. The order of the words helps you understand the idea. For instance, in the sentence "The cat bit Natalie," the subject is _the cat_. It is the thing that bit. We know that Natalie did not bite the cat! The order of the words in sentences is important.

2.　　We pronounce letters. The sound of the letters in a word is called the pronunciation. When you know a language, you know the sounds of the language. You know how to say the words. In English, the same sound can be made by different letters. For example, look at the words _alphabet_ and _funny_. Which letters make the /f/ sound? Pronunciation is one part of understanding a language.

3.　　We use language for speaking and writing. Many times when we talk, we don't use a complete sentence. However, we do use complete sentences in writing. What is a complete sentence? A complete sentence tells an idea. The words are in the right order. All sentences in English have a verb. The shortest sentence in English is one word. "Go!" How long is the longest sentence?

E. Match each group of sentences to the correct text from Activity D.

1. _____ You can always add ideas to sentences. For example, "I live in the house in the woods" can be "I live in the house in the woods by the mountains near the sea..."

2. _____ In addition, letters can make different sounds. The _s_ at the end of _sheets_ sounds like /s/, but at the end of _bowls_, it sounds like /z/.

3. _____ Not every sentence uses the same order. For example, questions can begin with a verb: "Are you OK?"

● Make Connections

Text to Self

When you make a connection to a text, you think about what you know.

A. Write a short answer to each question.

1. Does your language use letters?

_____

2. When do you use complete sentences?

_____

3. What is language?

_____

Text to Text

When you make connections between texts, you think about what they talk about. How are the texts the same? How are they different?

B. Look at the three paragraphs in Activity D on page 16. Complete each sentence with a word from the box.

language   order   pronunciation   sentences   sounds   write

1. The three texts talk about _____language_____ .

2. The first text talks about the _____ of the words in sentences.

3. The second text talks about the _____ of letters. This is called

   _____ .

4. The third text talks about using complete _____ . It's important to use

   complete sentences when we _____ .

Text to World

When you make a connection to the world, you think about the text and what you know about other texts, ideas, and writers in the world.

C. Answer the questions with a partner. Look at the Oxford 2000 keywords on page 133 and find words to help you.

1. Why do writers use complete sentences?

2. When is pronunciation important?

Look at the word bank for the Readiness Unit. Check (✓) the words you know. Circle the words you want to learn better.

OXFORD 2000 🔑					
Adjectives		**Nouns**		**Verbs**	
beautiful	hot	bathroom	letter	be (is/are)	look
big	interesting	bicycle	museum	dream	make
blue	new	clothes	musician	enter	meet
clean	old	coffee	ocean	examine	tell
dark	red	crowd	order	give	think
dirty	serious	family	pattern	go	work
happy	tall	female	phone	laugh	write
		forest	pronunciation		
		idea	sentence		
		language	sound		

PRACTICE WITH THE OXFORD 2000 🔑

A. Use the words in the chart. Match adjectives with nouns.

1. _____ new bicycle _____   2. _____

3. _____   4. _____

5. _____

B. Use the words in the chart. Match verbs with nouns.

1. _____ write letters _____   2. _____

3. _____   4. _____

5. _____

C. Use the words in the chart. Match verbs with adjective noun partners.

1. _____ think interesting ideas _____   2. _____

3. _____   4. _____

5. _____

UNIT **1** Present

UNIT WRAP UP   ## Extend Your Skills

What Influence Do Businesses Have on You?

- /s/, /z/, and /ɪz/ sounds
- Shortened forms of words
- Identify fact and opinion
- Simple present with *he/she*; frequency adverbs with *be*

▲ BEFORE READING ► Oxford 2000 🔑 words to talk about advertising

Learn Vocabulary

A. Match each picture to the correct phrase.

_____ an **advertisement** for shoes

_____ a hairstyling **service**

_____ a **product** in a store

_____ **buy** a tablet

__1__ **sell** a tablet

_____ **persuade** people to ride the bus

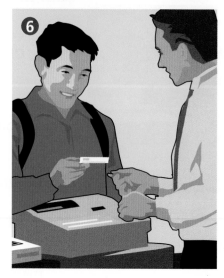

B. Match each picture to the correct phrase.

__1__ the **target** of an advertisement   ____ a **fact** about a car

____ have an **influence** on people   ____ an **opinion** about a car

Oxford 2000 🔑

Use the Oxford 2000 list on page 133 to find more words to describe the pictures on these pages. Share your words with a partner.

C. Complete each sentence with a word from the box.

advertisement	fact	opinion	product	service
buy	influence	persuade	sells	target

1. This is a(n) __advertisement__ for Luxor watches.

2. It is an advertisement for a(n) _____, not for a(n) _____.

3. The _____ of the advertisement is men.

4. You can _____ this watch at Kellman's Department Store.

5. Lane Jewelers also _____ this watch.

6. It is a(n) _____ that Luxor watches are made in France.

7. It is a(n) _____ that Luxor watches are beautiful.

8. The Luxor watch company wants to _____ people to buy its watches.

9. Do you think advertisements like this have a(n) _____ on you?

D. Discuss question 9 in Activity C with a partner.

GO ONLINE
for more practice

Preview the Text

E. Look at the text on page 24. Write a short answer to each question.

1. What is the title? _____

2. Where do you think this text is from? For example, is it from a magazine, a textbook, the Internet? _____

3. What do you think the purpose of the text is? For example, is it to inform, to persuade, to entertain? _____

F. Look at the text on page 24. Circle the correct answer.

1. What do you think the text will include?

   a. facts only   b. opinions only   c. both facts and opinions

2. What do you think the text will explain?

   a. reasons that some ads   b. ways that ads persuade   c. ways that advertisers
      are good   people to buy things   identify their targets

Sounds of English

Spelling Connection

A. There are three possible ending sounds for plural *s* and third person singular *s*: /s/, /z/, and /ɪz/. We say the /z/ sound after the voiced sounds like /b/, /g/, /l/, /r/, /w/, /v/, /m/, /n/, /y/, and all vowels. We say the /s/ sound after the voiceless sounds like /p/, /k/, /t/, and /f/. We say the /ɪz/ sound after /s/, /z/, /tʃ/, and /dʒ/ sounds. Listen to the examples.

/s/ *gets*   /z/ *ads*   /ɪz/ *watches*

B. Write each word on the correct line: *services, products, opinions*.

/s/ _____   /z/ _____   /ɪz/ _____

C. Listen to the words. Circle the ending sound that you hear.

1. opinions	a. /s/	b. /z/	c. /ɪz/
2. facts	a. /s/	b. /z/	c. /ɪz/
3. influences	a. /s/	b. /z/	c. /ɪz/
4. targets	a. /s/	b. /z/	c. /ɪz/
5. services	a. /s/	b. /z/	c. /ɪz/

⬤ Make Connections: Text to Self

A. Answer the questions.

1. How many advertisements do you think you see each day? _____

2. Where do you see these ads? _____

3. Do you remember any songs or slogans (phrases about a product or service that are easy to remember)? Write down some words to an advertisement song or a slogan that you remember.

_____

_____

B. Answer the questions with a partner.

1. Do you think most ads include more facts or opinions? Explain.

2. What is your favorite advertisement? What is one reason that you like it?

3. What is an advertisement that you don't like? What is one reason that you don't like it?

4. Do you watch TV ads or do you skip them? Why?

C. Think of a TV advertisement that you like. Complete the chart with information about the ad.

What Images Do You See?

_____

_____

_____

What Words Do You See?

_____

_____

_____

Product or Service

What Sounds Do You Hear?

_____

_____

_____

Why Do You Like the Ad?

_____

_____

_____

▲▲ DURING READING
► Vocabulary strategy: Shortened forms of words
► Reading strategy: Identify fact and opinion

🔊 Reading 1

A. Read the text on your own.

What Makes a Good Ad?

No one is sure how many **advertisements**, or ads, we see every day. However, some people think that we see about 250 ads each day. What do you think? Think about the ads that you see on TV, in magazines, on buildings, on the net, and on phone apps. One study showed that Internet users see more than 1,700 online ads each month. We don't really notice all 250 of these daily ads. There are a few reasons for this. One reason is we only notice ads for things that we are interested in. Another reason comes from scientific research: Researchers say it isn't possible for our brains to focus on everything we see. And a third reason is that some ads are better than others. So what makes a good ad?

First of all, a good ad gets people's attention. An ad can't have an **influence** on people if no one looks at it or watches it. An advertisement can get people's attention with an exciting photo, surprising **facts**, or an interesting story.

Second, a good ad reaches its **target** audience. Advertisers need to know who their target audience is and where it is. For example, the target audience of an ad for baby food is the parents of young children. Therefore, advertisers should find out what TV shows these parents watch, what magazines they read, and where they spend their time.

Finally, a good ad is always easy to remember. One way to make an ad easy to remember is to include a great slogan—a short phrase about a **product** or **service**. Another way is to include a fun song. People enjoy repeating slogans and singing fun songs, and that will help them remember an ad. An ad that gets people's attention, reaches its target audience, and is easy to remember can really help **sell** a product or **persuade** people to use a service.

Stop and Think

How many ads do you see a day? How many do you think you notice?

B. Certain words signal that the writer is presenting a new idea. Some examples of these words are *first, first of all, second, finally, one kind/way, another kind/ way,* **and** *a third type.* **Find and underline these words in the reading:** *first of all, second, finally.*

C. Where did you find the words—at the beginning, in the middle, or at the end of the paragraphs?

Check Your Understanding

D. Complete the chart with information from the reading on page 24.

Supporting Idea 1	Example or Detail
Good ads get people's _____ _____	An ad can include _____ _____

Blog Post Topic	Supporting Idea 2	Example or Detail
What Makes a Good Ad?	Good ads reach their _____ _____	Advertisers need to know what _____ _____ their target audience watches.

Supporting Idea 3	Example or Detail
Good ads are easy to _____ _____	Ads can include _____ _____

Vocabulary Strategy

Shortened Forms of Words

We often use shortened forms of words instead of full forms. Recognizing and understanding shortened forms of words is an easy way to build your vocabulary. Shortened words are usually made up of the first few letters or the last few letters of a word.

examination → exam   gasoline → gas   refrigerator → fridge

GO ONLINE for more practice

E. Match each word to its shortened form.

__d__ 1. advertisement   a. net

_____ 2. photograph   b. app

_____ 3. Internet   c. photo

_____ 4. telephone   ~~d. ad~~

_____ 5. application   e. phone

Identify Fact and Opinion

Facts are things that are true or that you can prove. *Opinions* are things that people think or believe. Identifying facts and opinions helps you respond to arguments in the texts you read.

Fact: *The first magazine advertisement appeared in 1742.*

Opinion: *There are too many advertisements in magazines.*

Writers often introduce facts with phrases like these:

research shows   *according to a recent study*   *one study showed*

They often introduce opinions with words like these:

think   *believe*   *opinion*   *should*

GO ONLINE
for more practice

F. Read each sentence from the reading on page 24. Circle *Fact* or *Opinion*.

1. However, some people think that we see about 250 ads each day.

   Fact   Opinion

2. One study showed that Internet users see over 1,700 online ads each month.

   Fact   Opinion

3. Another reason comes from scientific research: Researchers say it isn't possible for our brains to focus on everything we see.

   Fact   Opinion

4. Advertisers should find out what TV shows these parents watch, what magazines they read, and where they spend their time.

   Fact   Opinion

◎ Reading 2

A. Listen and read along.

How Does Targeted Advertising Work?

Do you notice a lot of **advertisements** for things that you like when you are online? That's because companies use targeted advertising to advertise **products** and **services** to people. How do advertisers know what you like? They collect data, or information, from you.

One kind of data that they collect is called *clickstream data*. This is information about the websites that you visit. Do you visit a lot of sites about health and exercise? Then you probably see a lot of ads for gyms and exercise clothes.

Another kind of useful data is *search data*. This is information about what you look for on a search engine. Studies show that over 90 percent of adults use search engines. When you do an online search, targeted ads appear next to your regular search results. For example, if you do research about a tablet, you will see advertisements for stores that **sell** tech items like tablets and laptops.

A third type of data that companies use is *purchase data*. This is information about what you buy. Companies find out what you **buy** online and try to sell you similar products. For instance, if you buy a book and a pair of shoes, you might see a combo of book ads and shoe ads.

A fourth kind of information is *profile data*. This is usually information that you include in your profile on social networks like Facebook and Twitter. This often includes your age, your city, your favorite books and music, and your other interests. Companies collect this info about you and make sure that you see ads targeted to people your age and with your interests. For example, consider a 20-year-old man. He lives in New York and plays the guitar; he will see ads for music stores in New York.

Is this kind of targeted advertising good or bad? Some people think it's great. Other people think it's always a bad idea. In their **opinion**, it's never OK to collect personal information about people. What do you think?

Stop and Think

Think about your social networking profiles. What kinds of information do you share? Do you want companies to know this information about you?

B. Find and underline the words in the reading that tell you that the writer is presenting a new idea.

Grammar in the Readings

Notice the simple present with *he/she* in the reading.

Regular simple present verbs with *he* and *she* end with *-s* or *-es*.

> <u>He</u> liv**es** in New York.   <u>He</u> play**s** the guitar.

Notice frequency adverbs with *be* in the readings.

Frequency adverbs (*always, usually, often, sometimes, never*) usually come after the verb *be* (*am, is, are*). Use *sometimes* after the verb *be* or at the beginning of a sentence.

> *A good ad **is always** easy to remember.*
> *In their opinion, **it's never** OK to collect personal information about people.*
> ***Sometimes** ads **are** funny.*
> *Ads **are sometimes** funny.*

GO ONLINE
for grammar practice

Check Your Understanding

C. Match each type of data with the correct description.

___b___ 1. clickstream data

_____ 2. search data

_____ 3. purchase data

_____ 4. profile data

a. things that you buy

~~b. websites that you visit~~

c. your information on social networking sites

d. information that you look for online

D. Identify each type of data, and write it on the line.

___purchase___ 1. You buy a pair of shoes and two pairs of pants online.

_____ 2. You are writing a paper for school and you search for information about Japan.

_____ 3. You want to take a vacation, so you check vacation prices online.

_____ 4. You are 20 years old and like to play video games.

Recycle

the Vocabulary Strategy

Vocabulary Strategy: Shortened Forms of Words

E. Find and underline the shortened form of each word in the reading on pages 26–27. Then write it on the line.

1. websites: _____sites_____

2. combination: _____

3. gymnasium: _____

4. information: _____

5. technology: _____

Recycle

the Reading Strategy

Reading Strategy: Identify Fact and Opinion

F. Read each sentence from the reading on pages 26–27. Circle *Fact* or *Opinion*.

1. They collect data, or information, from you.

   (Fact)   Opinion

2. This is information about the websites that you visit.

   Fact   Opinion

3. Then you probably see a lot of ads for gyms and exercise clothes.

   Fact   Opinion

4. Studies show that over 90 percent of adults use search engines.

   Fact   Opinion

5. In their opinion, it's never OK to collect personal information about people.

   Fact   Opinion

● Make Connections: Text to Text

A. Circle the correct answer.

1. Both readings in this chapter are about _____ .

   a. advertising   b. products and services

2. _____ explained why we see certain ads online.

   a. "What Makes a Good Ad?"   b. "How Does Targeted Advertising Work?"

3. _____ explained what makes some ads better than others.

   a. "What Makes a Good Ad?"   b. "How Does Targeted Advertising Work?"

4. Think about the information from "What Makes a Good Ad?" We probably _____ all of the ads that target us online.

   a. notice   b. don't notice

5. An advertisement that people remember is an example of a _____ ad.

   a. good   b. bad

B. Think about an ad that you saw when you were online. Then complete the chart with information about the ad.

What was the ad for?	
How did it get your attention?	
Why was it easy to remember?	
Do you think the advertisers targeted you with the ad? Why or why not?	

Summarizing and Retelling

A. Complete the sentences with the words from the box. Some of the words have to be changed to fit the sentences. For example, *advertisement* has to be changed to *advertisements*. Then read the sentences with a partner to summarize.

Nouns	Verbs
advertisement	buy
fact	persuade
influence	sell
opinion	
product	
service	
target	

1. Companies use _____ to try to _____ things to people.

2. These ads show different _____ like smart phones, cars, and snack foods.

3. They also show _____ like healthcare or housecleaning.

4. Companies make these advertisements because they want to _____ people to _____ their products and services.

5. Sometimes companies use _____ in their advertisements. For example, a car ad might include information about the price of the car.

6. Companies want people to remember their advertisements because ads can have an _____ on people only if people remember them.

7. Companies also want the right people to see their ads. Therefore, they need to know who their _____ audience is.

8. A lot of companies make online ads. Only certain people see these ads. The companies find out personal information about people and send them specific ads. Some people think that it's wrong to find out people's personal information. What's your _____ about this issue?

Word Partners

have an influence on

a good influence

a bad influence

a strong influence

a positive influence

a negative influence

GO ONLINE
to practice
word partners

B. Think about the two texts. Answer the questions.

1. What are three things that make a good ad?

_____

_____

2. What are four types of data that companies use for targeted marketing?

_____

_____

Make Connections: Text to World

A. Find a magazine ad. Answer the questions with a partner.

1. What is the ad trying to sell?

2. Who is the target of the ad?

3. Does the ad include any facts about the product or service? What are they?

4. Does the ad include any opinions about the product or service? What are they?

5. Do you think it's a good ad? Why or why not?

B. Find a targeted online ad. Answer the questions with a partner.

1. What is the ad trying to sell?

2. Why do you think the company targeted you with this ad?

3. Do you think the ad can persuade you to buy a product or service? Why or why not?

C. Think about the two texts. Answer the questions with a partner.

1. What kinds of ads have the most influence on you: TV ads, online ads, magazine ads, or ads you see on cars or buildings? Explain.

2. In your opinion, is targeted advertising good or bad? Why?

3. Imagine that you want to sell a product. What kind of ad is best for you: a TV ad, an online ad, a magazine ad, or an ad on a car or building? Why?

Chant

GO ONLINE
for the
Chapter 1
Vocabulary &
Grammar Chant

CHAPTER 2

Is Online Communication Always Good?

- Syllable stress
- Use a dictionary
- Identify viewpoints and opinions
- Simple present with frequency adverbs; verbs with *to*

▲ BEFORE READING ► Oxford 2000 ✎ words to talk about communication

Learn Vocabulary

A. Match each picture to the correct sentence.

_____ You can use emoticons to show **emotions** such as happy or sad.

_____ Someone hit Jack's car. He is **angry**.

_____ I like to take pictures of my friends and **post** them online.

_____ It's **polite** to hold a door open for someone.

_____ It's **rude** to look at your phone when you are having dinner with your family.

__1__ Don't stay home alone all the time. Be **social** and do things with your friends.

B. Match each picture to the correct sentence.

_____ If something is **useful**, it makes life easier.

__1__ If something is **immediate**, you don't have to wait for it.

_____ If you **reply** to a text, you write to someone after he or she writes to you.

_____ If you **complain** about something, you tell someone that you are unhappy about it.

C. Complete the email with the words from the box. You will not use three of the words.

angry	emotions	polite	reply	social
complain	~~immediate~~	post	rude	useful

Oxford 2000 🔑

Use the Oxford 2000 list on page 133 to find more words to describe the pictures on these pages. Share your words with a partner.

Dear Store Manager,

I shop in your store every week. I really like your store. Your salespeople are friendly, and I usually get ____immediate____ help. I don't have to wait. However, last week, I had a bad experience at your store.

I'm writing to _____ about one of your employees. I went to your store last week to look at laptops. I wanted to talk to a salesperson, but I had to wait a long time. After about 20 minutes, your employee Sam started to help me. At first, he was _____. He answered all of my questions, and he showed me several laptops. But when I couldn't decide, he got very _____. He stopped answering my questions and walked away from me. I felt really _____, so I left.

There are other stores in town, but I like to go to your store because it's close to my house and my job. It's very _____. I hope we can find a solution to this problem. Please _____ to my email soon.

Best regards,
Mina Geller

GO ONLINE
for more practice

Preview the Text

D. Look at the text on page 36. Write a short answer to each question.

1. What is the title? _____

2. List ways that people communicate online.

_____

_____

E. In your opinion, what are some differences and similarities between online communication and in-person communication? Complete the Venn diagram with your own ideas.

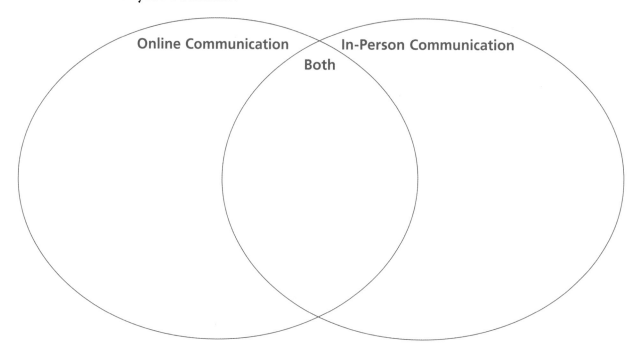

Online Communication   In-Person Communication

Both

Sounds of English

Spelling Connection

🔊 A. Every word in English has one *stressed* syllable. That means one syllable is pronounced longer and louder than the other syllables. Listen to these examples:

    on•LINE   *po•LITE*   *SO•cial*   *com•MU•ni•cate*

🔊 B. Listen to the words. Circle the stressed syllable of each word.

    re•ply   an•gry   e•mo•tion   im•me•di•ate   nec•es•sar•y

⚫ Make Connections: Text to Self

A. Answer the questions.

1. What kinds of online communication do you use?

_____

2. What is your favorite form of online communication? Why is it your favorite?

_____

_____

3. What is your *least* favorite form of online communication? Why do you dislike it?

_____

_____

B. How do you communicate with different people in your life? Complete the chart.

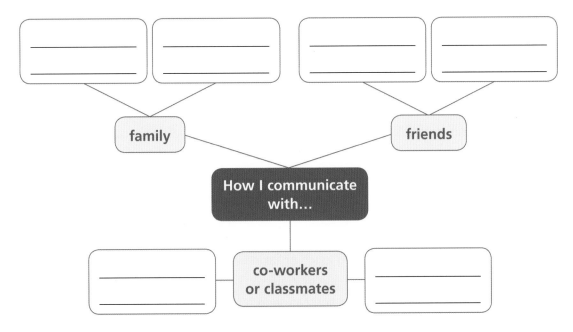

C. Answer the questions with a partner.

1. Do you prefer online communication or face-to-face communication? Why?

2. When is online communication better than face-to-face communication?

3. When is face-to-face communication better than online communication?

▲▲ DURING READING
▶ Vocabulary strategy: Use a dictionary
▶ Reading strategy: Identify viewpoints and opinions

◉ Reading 1

A. Read the text on your own.

What Are the Characteristics of Online Communication?

Everywhere you go, you see people texting, sending emails, and **posting** thoughts and photos to **social** networks. Of course, this kind of online communication isn't the same as in-person communication. There are several important differences.

When you talk to people face-to-face, you can see them. Their faces and the way they move their bodies can tell you about their emotions. Imagine that you are having coffee with a friend. Your friend says, "I have something to tell you." If your friend is smiling, you know the news is good. If your friend looks sad, you know the news is bad. When you communicate by text message or email, you can't see these clues. You can use emoticons, such as ☺ or ☹, but these are very informal. You can't use these in more formal communications, such as emails to your professor or your employer.

You can hear a person's voice when you talk in person. Again, this helps you understand how the other person feels. Does the person sound **angry**? Is the person making a joke? Does the person sound **polite** or **rude**? With online communication such as emails and texts, it's easy to misunderstand someone's feelings because you can't hear their voice.

We usually keep online communication brief and to the point. In other words, people often use text messages, emails, and social networking posts to communicate short messages. When you talk to someone face-to-face, you are more likely to talk about several different topics and develop new ideas as you communicate. You can also do an activity together, such as having lunch or taking a walk.

Do you prefer to communicate online or in person? Communicating online is great for some situations. It's also quick and you can send a text or email when you want, even when the other person is sleeping. However, in-person communication allows you to understand a person's **emotions**. It also lets you build relationships because you can do **social** activities while you talk.

Stop and Think

Think of a time when a friend told you happy news. What facial expressions and body language did your friend use?

B. Listen to the text. In the first paragraph, underline the stressed syllable in each word with two or more syllables.

C. Now take turns reading the text with a partner.

Check Your Understanding

D. Complete the chart with information from the reading on page 36.

Differences between Online Communication and In-Person Communication

Online Communication	In-Person Communication
can't see emotions	

E. Write a short answer to each question.

1. What types of online communication does the writer mention? _____ *texting,* _____

_____

2. What is an example of an emoticon? _____

3. When should you not use an emoticon? _____

_____

4. Why is it easy to misunderstand someone's tone in an email? _____

_____

GO ONLINE
for more
practice

Vocabulary Strategy

Use a Dictionary

Using a dictionary helps you understand new words. Dictionaries have definitions, but they also have other information about words. Look at this dictionary entry for the word *reply.*

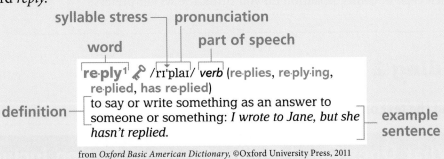

syllable stress — pronunciation

word   part of speech

re·ply¹ 🔑 /rɪˈplaɪ/ *verb* (re·plies, re·ply·ing, re·plied, has re·plied)

definition — to say or write something as an answer to someone or something: *I wrote to Jane, but she hasn't replied.* — example sentence

from *Oxford Basic American Dictionary,* ©Oxford University Press, 2011

F. Use a dictionary to find a definition for the word *prefer.*

_____

_____

G. Write a short answer to each question about the dictionary entry for *prefer.*

1. What is the pronunciation? _____

2. What is the part of speech? _____

3. Which syllable is stressed? _____

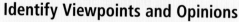

Identify Viewpoints and Opinions

Writers often have certain viewpoints and opinions about their topics. Figuring out the writer's viewpoint or opinion can help you better understand what you are reading. Sometimes writers use phrases that introduce an opinion.

in my opinion   *I think*   *I believe*

Other times, you need to read carefully to understand the writer's viewpoint. For example, when comparing two things, the writer might discuss the good points of one thing and the bad points of the second thing. That means the writer prefers the first thing.

GO ONLINE
for more
practice

H. The writer says some positive and negative, or good and bad, things about online communication and face-to-face communication. List the positive details from your chart on page 36.

1. Facial expressions and body language tell you about emotions.

2. _____

3. _____

4. _____

5. _____

I. Look at your answers in Activity H. Write a short answer to each question.

1. Are these positive details about online communication or in-person communication?

_____

2. Which type of communication do you think the writer prefers?

_____

◉ Reading 2

A. Read the text on your own.

What Does Good Online Communication Include?

Stop and Think

Before you read, what do you think good online communication should include?

A lot of communication happens online. Online communication has to be clear and easy to understand. This is especially important for emails because we often send emails to professors, employers, and co-workers. Here are some tips for good email communication:

1. Check your message for mistakes before you send it. One benefit of online communication is that it isn't **immediate**. That means that you can correct mistakes like spelling errors or extra spaces between words. Small errors can look bad. Big errors can make

your message hard to understand.

2. Make sure that your email is complete before you send it. Did you forget any important details? Did you ask all your questions? No one likes to receive ten emails about the same thing. Read your email and add any missing information.

3. It's important to include all the necessary information. However, keep your emails short. Studies show that people don't always read long emails. Sometimes they save long emails and read them when they have a lot of time. Sometimes they just delete long emails and don't read them at all. Make sure that your whole email fits on a computer screen.

4. **Reply** to emails quickly. Email is a **useful** way to communicate because you can get answers quickly. People expect to receive replies one or two days after they send an email. If you don't have time to write a reply quickly, you can send an email that says, "I received your message. I can't reply today, but I will send a reply before Friday."

5. Remember that email can last forever and it can be shared. Therefore, think carefully before you send an email. If you are **angry**, wait 24 hours before you send an email. If you want to **complain** about a co-worker, be careful. Don't complain to co-workers or friends. Send an email to your boss, but be **polite**. Do not type in ALL CAPS or use more than one exclamation point.

Email is a very convenient way to communicate. In fact, I believe it's one of the best ways to communicate. However, there can be problems if you are not careful.

B. Circle the stressed syllable in each word below.

1. es•pe•cial•ly

2. em•ploy•ers

3. for•ev•er

4. mis•takes

5. de•lete

Grammar in the Readings

Notice the simple present with frequency adverbs in the readings.

Frequency adverbs usually come before verbs other than *be*. *Sometimes* can come before a subject or a verb.

> We **usually** keep online communication brief and to the point.
> People **often** use text messages, emails, and social networking posts to communicate short messages.
> People **sometimes** communicate online only and never talk in person.
> **Sometimes** people communicate online only and never talk in person.

Notice verbs with *to* in the readings.

We use *to* + a verb after certain verbs.

> I **like to text** my friends.   I **prefer to communicate** in person.
> I **try to call** my parents once a week.
> I always **offer to help** my neighbor with her computer.

GO ONLINE
for grammar
practice

Check Your Understanding

C. Complete each sentence with information from the reading on pages 38–39.

1. You check your email for mistakes before you send it because mistakes can make your email hard to understand.

2. You should make sure your email is complete because _____

_____

3. You should keep your emails short because _____

_____

4. If you can't reply to an email immediately, you should _____

_____

5. You should think carefully and wait before you send an angry email because

_____

D. Answer the questions with a partner.

1. Which tip do you think is the most important? Why?

2. Do you follow these tips when you send email? Why or why not?

Recycle

the Vocabulary Strategy

Vocabulary Strategy: Use a Dictionary

E. Choose a word from the reading on pages 38–39 that you don't know. Write a short answer to each question about the word.

1. What is the pronunciation? _____

2. What is the part of speech? _____

3. What is the definition? _____

4. Which syllable is stressed? _____

Recycle

the Reading Strategy

Reading Strategy: Identify Viewpoints and Opinions

F. Find each word in the reading on pages 38–39. Write the sentence that includes the word.

1. benefit _____

2. convenient _____

3. useful _____

4. believe _____

G. Answer the questions about the sentences in Activity F.

1. Are these positive or negative details about email communication? _____

_____

2. Do you think the writer likes or dislikes email? _____

_____

⬤ Make Connections: Text to Text

A. Circle the correct answer.

1. Both readings in this chapter are about _____ .

   a. communication   b. texting

2. _____ gave tips for good online communication.

   a. Reading 1   b. Reading 2

3. _____ compared two types of communication.

   a. Reading 1   b. Reading 2

4. Think about the information from "What Does Good Online Communication Include?" It does not include a tip for _____ .

   a. expressing emotions in email   b. replying to emails quickly

5. The two writers have _____ opinions about online communication.

   a. the same   b. different

B. Answer the questions with a partner.

1. Think about the tips in "What Does Good Online Communication Include?" Can you use any of these tips for texting? Social networking posts?

2. Think of one additional tip for good texting and one additional tip for good social networking posts.

3. Besides emoticons, how do you think you can you show emotion in an email, text, or online post?

4. What do you do when you think a text message from a friend sounds rude?

Summarizing and Retelling

A. Complete the sentences with the words from the box. Then read the paragraphs to a partner to summarize.

Adjectives		Nouns	Verbs
angry	rude	emotion	complain
immediate	social		post
polite	useful		reply

1. Email is very _____ because you can get answers from people quickly.

2. Online communication is not _____. You have time to check your message before you send it.

3. If you want to _____ about a co-worker, email your boss. Don't email other co-workers.

4. You can show _____ in face-to-face communication, but it's difficult in online communication.

5. You should wait 24 hours before you send an email if you feel _____. Wait until you feel calm.

6. When you are talking to someone in person, you can see if they're being

   _____ or rude.

7. People send text messages and _____ ideas on social networking sites all day long.

8. Be sure to _____ quickly to emails. Don't wait more than two days.

9. Sometimes a text message sounds _____ even when the person is trying to be nice.

10. You can do a(n) _____ activity with a friend when you talk in person.

B. Which ideas go with each text? Write the number of each sentence in Activity A in the Venn diagram.

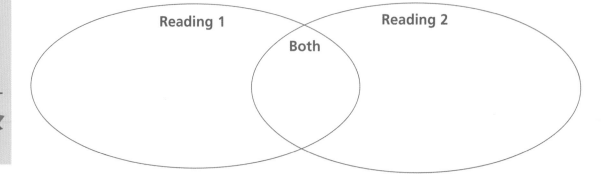

Word Partners

online communication

in-person communication

formal communication

face-to-face communication

email communication

GO ONLINE ▲▲▲
to practice
word partners ▼▼▼

● Make Connections: Text to World

A. Read each situation. Identify the problem, and write it below. Then share your answers with a partner.

1. Boris gets an email from a classmate on Monday. He reads the email, but he doesn't have time to reply immediately. He emails the classmate back on Friday.

_____

2. Marissa sends an email to her friend Kim. It says, "I can't have dinner with you tonight." Kim replies, "Did I do something wrong?"

_____

3. Elena had a job interview yesterday. She sends a thank-you email to the interviewer. She signs it, "Sincerely, Elena Sung ☺".

_____

4. Matthew has some important information to share with his co-workers. He sends them an email. It is two pages long. No one reads it.

_____

5. Kevin went shopping yesterday. The salesperson at a store was rude to him. He sends an email to the store manager to complain. In the email, he says, "Pleas send an imediate reply."

_____

6. Lara wants to ask her professor a few questions. She sends an email with three questions. Two minutes later, she remembers another question, and she sends another email.

_____

B. Read the email from Alexandra and think about how she feels. Then talk about your ideas with a partner.

Hi Susanna,

    Do you have my red sweater? I wanted to wear it yesterday, but it wasn't in my closet. I know you like to borrow my clothes, and that's OK. But can you please return my red sweater? It's my favorite one.

Thanks,

Alexandra

> **Chant**
>
> **GO ONLINE**
> for the
> Chapter 2
> Vocabulary &
> Grammar Chant

Why Do We Have Sports?

- Intonation with *yes/no* and information questions
- Word families
- Identify examples
- *have/has to* + verb

▲ **BEFORE READING** ▶ Oxford 2000 ⚷ words to talk about sports

Learn Vocabulary

A. Look at the pictures and read the sentences.

1. When you **play** a game, you are part of the game. When you **watch** a game, you are not part of it.

2. If something is **enjoyable**, it's fun.

3. Some people like all kinds of **sports**. For **example**, they like tennis and snowboarding.

4. If you **finish** something, you reach the end of it.

B. Look at the picture. Use the bold words from Activity A to label the parts. You will not use all the words.

enjoyable

RACE

C. Match each picture to the correct description.

_____ If you are **successful**, you win or do what you hoped to do.

We were successful. We won our game.

<u>1</u> If you are in a **competition**, you try to win a game against someone else.

I play sports because I like competition. I like to try to win.

_____ Your **health** is your physical condition.

Eating vegetables is good for your health.

_____ A **community** is a group of people who live in one place or are connected in some way.

I live in a great community. We work together to keep our parks clean.

Preview the Text

D. Look at the picture on page 48. Write a short answer to each question.

1. What is the person doing?

_____

2. How do you think the person feels?

_____

3. Do you think the person is enjoying herself or not? How do you know?

_____

E. Look at the text on page 48. Write a short answer to each question.

1. What is the title? _____

2. Where do you think this text is from? For example, is it from a magazine, a textbook, the Internet?

_____

3. Does the text seem very serious, a little serious, or funny?

_____

Sounds of English

Spelling Connection

A. Information questions end with falling intonation. This means that the speaker's voice goes down at the end of the question. *Yes/No* questions end in rising intonation. The speaker's voice goes up at the end of the question. Listen to these examples.

Information question: *Why do people play sports?*

Yes/No question: *Do you play sports?*

B. Listen to the questions. Circle the correct type of question.

1. Do you play baseball?
   a. information question   b. *yes/no* question

2. What's your favorite team?
   a. information question   b. *yes/no* question

3. Where do you play?
   a. information question   b. *yes/no* question

4. Do you want to play tennis?
   a. information question   b. *yes/no* question

5. Is Mark on this team?
   a. information question   b. *yes/no* question

● Make Connections: Text to Self

A. Answer the questions.

1. Do you play sports? Why or why not?

_____

_____

2. What kind of exercise do you like to do?

_____

_____

3. Why do you think people play sports? Write three ideas.

_____

_____

4. What do you think are some benefits, or good things, of playing sports? Write three ideas.

_____

_____

5. Think of the first sport that you ever played. How did you feel when you played?

_____

_____

B. What does the word *sports* make you think of? What does it make you feel? Write your ideas in the chart.

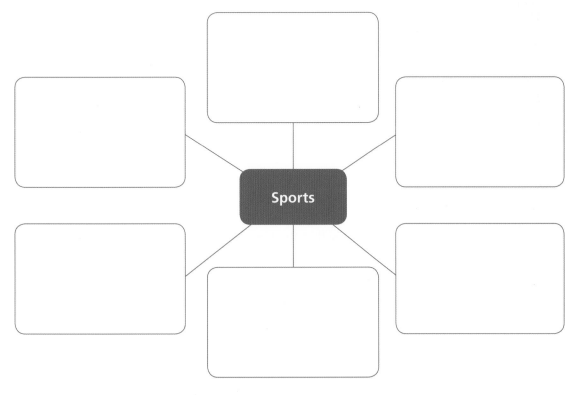

Sports

▲▲ DURING READING
▶ Vocabulary strategy: Word families
▶ Reading strategy: Identify examples

◑ Reading 1

A. Read the text on your own. Underline *yes/no* questions. Circle information questions.

Why Do People Play Sports?

Tennis, basketball, soccer, swimming—these are **examples** of the hundreds, maybe thousands, of **sports** in the world. People in every country in the world **play** some kind of athletic game. Why do people spend so much time and energy playing sports? It may be because playing sports has a lot of advantages.

Good **health** is one big advantage to playing sports. Exercise can make people stronger and help them live longer lives. For example, scientists in Finland recently did a study on identical twins. In these pairs of twins, one twin played some kind of sports and the other twin did not. The researchers discovered that the exercising twins had more muscle, more energy, and healthier hearts and lungs. The twins who did not play any sports had less energy and more fat.

> ### Stop and Think
> Why do you think the scientists studied twins and not other pairs of people?

Good health is not the only reason that people play sports. Another reason is because they want to be social. Sports allow people to spend time with friends and meet new people. For instance, people who play on a team become friends with their team members and meet players from different teams. Sports games become **enjoyable** social events, not just **competitions**.

An additional reason that people play sports is that it makes them feel good. It does this in two interesting ways. First, studies show that playing sports gives people self-esteem. In other words, it makes them feel good about themselves. For example, winning a tennis match can make a person feel **successful**. **Finishing** a long race can make someone feel confident. Second, research says that when we exercise, our brains make chemicals that make us feel good. As an example, when people run around for two hours playing a basketball game, they often feel great even if they lose the game.

There are a lot of other reasons why people play sports, but studies show that the biggest reason is enjoyment. When researchers asked a group of people why they play sports, most people said they play because it's fun. They don't have to play— they want to play. Do you want to be healthy, socialize, feel good, and have fun? Play a sport.

B. Read the text on page 48 again. As you read it a second time, check your understanding and see if you discover anything new.

Check Your Understanding

C. Write four reasons why people play sports.

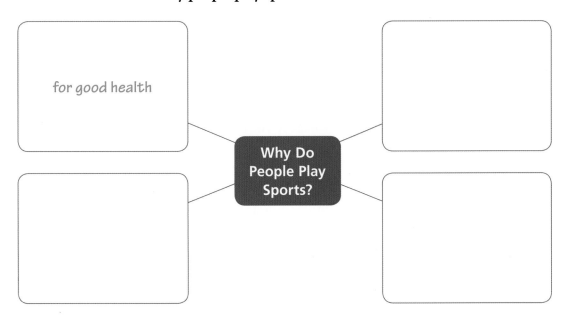

for good health

Why Do People Play Sports?

Vocabulary Strategy

Word Families
Word families are groups of words that have the same base word. The words in word families are usually different parts of speech. Learning word families instead of single words can help you learn a large amount of vocabulary quickly. Look at the examples.

noun: *success*   verb: *succeed*   adjective: *successful*

D. Complete the chart with words from the text on page 48.

Nouns	Verbs	Adjectives
_____health_____		healthy / healthful
Interest	_____	_____ / interested
science / _____		scientific
_____	compete	competitive

GO ONLINE
for more
practice

Identify Examples

Writers give examples to help readers understand what they are describing. Identifying when a writer is introducing an example helps you read more quickly. They often introduce these examples with phrases like these:

for example	*for instance*	*as an example*
such as	*like*	*these are a few examples*

E. Look at the text on page 48. Find and underline an example for each statement or phrase. Write the item number next to the underlined example.

1. hundreds, maybe thousands, of sports in the world

2. Exercise can make people stronger and help them live longer lives.

3. Sports allow people to spend time with friends and meet new people.

4. First, studies show that playing sports gives people self-esteem.

5. Second, research has discovered that when we exercise, our brains make chemicals that make us feel good.

◀) Reading 2

A. Listen and read along.

Why Do People Watch Sports?

Do you like to **watch** sports? A lot of people in the world do. Today, there are about 7 billion people on Earth. In 2014, 1 billion of them watched the final World Cup soccer match on television. That's 14 percent of the world's population! Every day, people watch sports on television, go to professional sports events, and watch local teams **play** against each other. Why do so many people watch sports events like soccer, baseball, and tennis?

One reason is that people can feel like they're in the game when they watch. Scientists studied people's brains to see what happens when people watch **sports**. They found that brain cells called "mirror neurons"

help people understand other people's actions and feel the emotions that the others are probably feeling. For instance, if a person watches a snowboarder fly into the air, the person might feel the excitement that the snowboarder feels. Mirror neurons allow people to feel the benefits of playing sports even when they're sitting on their sofas in their living rooms. They don't even have to move.

The human brain helps people enjoy watching sports for another reason, too. When a person's team or favorite athlete wins a **competition**, the person's brain releases a chemical. This chemical gives the person a feeling of happiness. As an **example**, sports fans yell, cheer, cry, and hug each other when they see their favorite team win a big game.

Being sports fans can also make people feel like they are part of a **community**. When people go to sports events and sit with other fans, they feel like they belong to a group. They don't even have to know the other fans. This feeling is important for humans. Humans are social animals and have to be around other people. They can get that feeling when they do activities in groups, such as cheering for their favorite teams.

Watching sports has a lot of benefits. If you're not a sports fan, watch a game or two. You might like it.

Stop and Think

When do you feel like you're doing an activity that you are actually only watching?

Grammar in the Readings

Notice *have/has to* + verb in the readings.

Use *have/has to* + verb to show that something is necessary or important to do.

> They **have to** eat good foods, such as fruits and vegetables.
> She **has to** watch her son play basketball tonight.

Use *do not (don't)/does not (doesn't)* + *have to* + verb to show that something is not necessary.

> They **don't have to** play—they want to play.
> They **don't have** to move.

GO ONLINE
for grammar practice

Check Your Understanding

B. Write three reasons why people watch sports.

Why Do People Watch Sports?

Reason 1	Reason 2	Reason 3
people feel like		
they are playing		

Vocabulary Strategy: Word Families

C. Circle the correct word to complete each sentence.

1. I play sports because I like to _____.

   (a. compete *(v.)*)   b. competition *(n.)*   c. competitive *(adj.)*

2. Marco is a great soccer _____.

   a. play *(v.)*   b. player *(n.)*   c. play *(n.)*

3. I _____ swimming and running.

   a. enjoy *(v.)*   b. enjoyable *(adj.)*   c. enjoyment *(n.)*

4. Did you _____ in the race?

   a. compete *(v.)*   b. competitive *(adj.)*   c. competition *(n.)*

5. We were not _____. We didn't win the game.

   a. success *(n.)*   b. succeed *(v.)*   c. successful *(adj.)*

Reading Strategy: Identify Examples

D. Look at the text on pages 50–51. Find and underline an example for each statement or phrase. Write the item number next to your underlined example in Reading 2.

1. brain cells called mirror neurons help people understand other people's actions and feel the emotions that the others are probably feeling.

2. When a person's team or favorite athlete wins a competition, the person's brain releases a chemical. This chemical gives the person a feeling of happiness.

3. do activities in groups

4. sports events

● Make Connections: Text to Text

A. Read each sentence. Does it describe Reading 1, Reading 2, or both? Write the letter of each sentence in the Venn diagram.

a. Mirror neurons make you feel like you're part of the game.

b. The brain makes chemicals that make us feel good and happy.

c. Exercise can make people strong.

d. Sports make people feel successful and confident.

e. Sports let people be social.

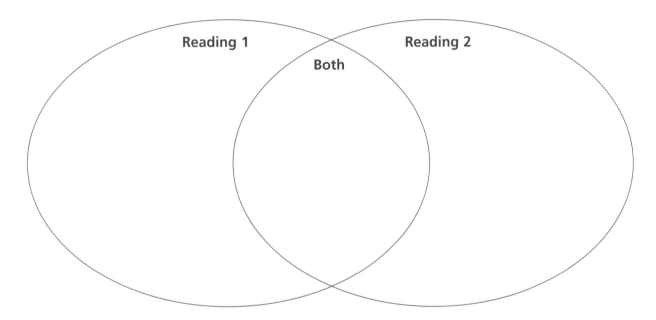

Reading 1   Both   Reading 2

B. What is each person talking about: playing sports or watching sports? Read each explanation and write *P* for *playing* or *W* for *watching*. Underline the words that helped you choose an answer.

1. _____ Why do I do it? First, I do it because it's a lot of fun. I spend time with my friends, and we cheer for our favorite teams. We talk to each other, and everybody brings good food to eat. We have a great time.

2. _____ I moved to this city five years ago, and I didn't know anyone. I started going to baseball games, and I enjoyed it a lot. I met a few people and made some new friends. Being a fan of my city's sports team makes me feel like part of a community.

3. _____ I always feel great after a game. I feel happy and self-confident, and it helps me stay healthy. Also, I really like the people on my team. I have a few friends on other teams, too. They're all really nice people. After a game, we usually go out for lunch or coffee.

Summarizing and Retelling

A. Complete the sentences with the words from the box. Then read the sentences to a partner to summarize.

Nouns	Verbs	Adjectives
community competition example health sports	finish play watch	enjoyable successful

1. Playing _____ is good for your _____ . It can make you stronger. If you _____ a sport a few times a week, you get a lot of exercise.

2. Winning a game or finishing a race can make you feel _____ . For _____ , if you _____ a 10-kilometer run, you feel like you did something important.

3. Everybody wants to win, but a game is not simply a(n) _____ . It's a way for friends to spend time together. It's also fun and _____ .

4. It's good to _____ sports with other people, even if the game is on television. It helps you feel like part of a(n) _____ .

B. Answer the questions with a partner.

1. Do you think that everyone who plays sports likes to watch sports? Do you think that everyone who watches sports likes to play sports? Explain your answers.

2. Which do you think has more benefits: playing sports or watching sports? Why?

Word Partners

watch a game

watch a DVD

watch TV

watch how I do this

watch me

watch out

GO ONLINE to practice word partners

⬤ Make Connections: Text to World

A. Answer the questions.

1. Which do you think is more enjoyable: playing sports or watching sports? Why?

_____

_____

2. Some sports are more difficult to play than others. What are three sports that you think are difficult to play? Explain.

_____

_____

_____

3. What are three sports that you think are easy to play? Explain.

_____

_____

_____

4. Besides sports, what are some other activities that:

are good for your health? _____

make you feel like part of a community? _____

are fun? _____

make you feel confident? _____

encourage people to compete with each other? _____

B. Talk about your answers from Activity A with a partner. Look at the Oxford 2000 keywords on page 133 and find five words to help you.

Chant

GO ONLINE
for the
Chapter 3
Vocabulary &
Grammar Chant

Look at the word bank for Unit 1. Check (✓) the words you know. Circle the words you want to learn better.

OXFORD 2000 🗝		
Adjectives	**Nouns**	**Verbs**
angry	advertisement	buy
enjoyable	community	complain
immediate	competition	finish
polite	emotion	persuade
rude	example	play
social	fact	post
successful	health	reply
useful	influence	sell
	opinion	watch
	product	
	service	
	sport	

PRACTICE WITH THE OXFORD 2000 🗝

A. Use the words in the chart. Match adjectives with nouns.

1. _____useful service_____   2. _____

3. _____   4. _____

5. _____

B. Use the words in the chart. Match verbs with nouns.

1. _____buy a product_____   2. _____

3. _____   4. _____

5. _____

C. Use the words in the chart. Match verbs with adjective noun partners.

1. _watch enjoyable competitions_   2. _____

3. _____   4. _____

5. _____

UNIT 2 Past

Has Exercise Always Been Important?

- Past tense /d/, /t/, and /ɪd/ sounds
- Descriptive adjectives
- Identify cause and effect
- Irregular past tense verbs

▲ BEFORE READING ▶ Oxford 2000 ⚷ words to talk about exercise

Learn Vocabulary

A. Match each picture to the correct description.

_____ A **cause** makes something happen.

The cause of the fire was a candle.

__1__ An **effect** is the result of something.

Eating well is having a positive effect on my health.

_____ If someone is **fit**, he or she is healthy.

Erica exercises a lot. She's really fit.

_____ **Evidence** is proof or shows that something is true.

We found evidence that there was a house here in the past.

1.

2.

3.

4.

B. Look at each picture. Complete each sentence with a word from the box.

| calm | ~~nervous~~ | include | ancient | energy | modern |

1.

When you are ___nervous___, you are worried. You don't feel relaxed.

2.

When you are _____, you feel relaxed.

3.

When you don't have a lot of _____, you feel tired and you don't want to do anything.

4.

If you _____ someone, you invite that person to join you.

5.

If something is _____, it is extremely old.

6.

If something is _____, it is of the present or recent times.

C. Complete the paragraph with the words from the box. You won't use two of the words.

| calm | ~~cause~~ | effects | energy | fit | modern | nervous |

Do you feel tired in the afternoon? Many different things can ___cause___ sleepiness during the day. A big lunch, a sugary snack, or sitting for a long time can make you tired. When you feel tired in the afternoon, don't drink coffee. It's true that coffee can have positive _____. For example, it can give you _____. However, too much coffee can make you feel _____. Instead, take a walk. That way, you can wake up and get _____ at the same time.

Oxford 2000 🔑

Use the Oxford 2000 list on page 133 to find more words to describe the pictures on these pages. Share your words with a partner.

GO ONLINE for more practice

Preview the Text

D. Look at the picture on page 62. Write a short answer to each question.

1. What is the person doing?

_____

2. What time period do you think the person is from?

_____

3. Who do you think the text is for: students, doctors, history professors, a
   general audience?

_____

E. Look at the text on page 62. Write a short answer to each question.

1. What is the title?

_____

2. Where do you think this text is from? For example, is it from a magazine, a textbook,
   the Internet?

_____

3. Who do you think the text is for: students, doctors, history professors, a general
   audience?

_____

Sounds of English

Spelling Connection

A. There are three possible ending sounds for regular past tense verbs: /d/, /t/,
and /ɪd/. We say the /d/ sound after the voiced sounds like /b/, /g/, /v/, /z/,
/m/, /n/, /l/, and all vowels. We say the /t/ sound after the voiceless sounds
like /p/, /k/, /s/, and /f/. We say the /ɪd/ sound after /t/ and /d/ sounds. Listen
to the examples.

/d/	/t/	/ɪd/
played	liked	wanted
called	missed	decided

B. Listen to the simple past verbs. Circle the ending sound that you hear.

1. worked   a. /d/   b. /t/   c. /ɪd/
2. invented   a. /d/   b. /t/   c. /ɪd/
3. used   a. /d/   b. /t/   c. /ɪd/
4. started   a. /d/   b. /t/   c. /ɪd/
5. cared   a. /d/   b. /t/   c. /ɪd/

⬤ Make Connections: Text to Self

A. Answer the questions.

1. When do you think exercise started to become popular? _____

_____

2. How often do you exercise? _____

_____

3. What do you think the first exercises were? _____

_____

4. Think of the kinds of exercise people do today. Which of these do you think people did

100 years ago? One thousand years ago? _____

_____

_____

B. What kinds of exercise can you do with other people? By yourself? Either? List
as many different kinds of exercise as you can in the Venn diagram.

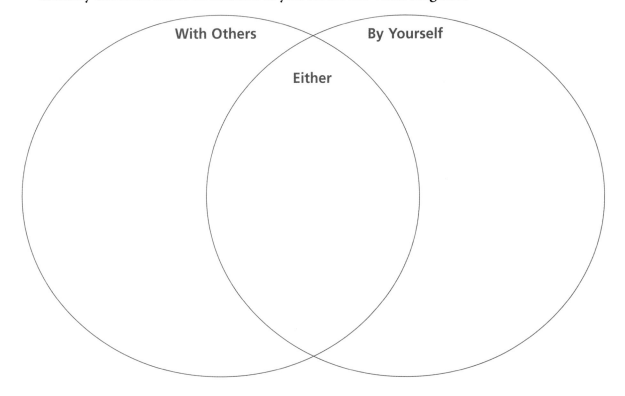

With Others   By Yourself

Either

▲▲ DURING READING
▶ Vocabulary strategy: Descriptive adjectives
▶ Reading strategy: Identify cause and effect

◑ Reading 1

A. Read the text. If you don't understand something, look back and ahead a few words to see if that makes the meaning clearer.

Did People in the Past Exercise?

Exercise is a part of many people's lives today. Many people swim, work out at gyms, or play sports several times a week because they want to be physically **fit**. But **modern** people didn't invent exercise. Was exercise popular in the past? The answer is yes! Exercise for physical fitness wasn't as popular in the past as it is today. However, people have been interested in exercise for thousands of years.

No one knows exactly when humans began to exercise, but we do know that exercise was very important in certain **ancient** civilizations. In ancient China, people knew that physical activity could help them stay healthy. So sometime between the 17th century BCE and 250 BCE, kung fu was invented in China. Today, people practice kung fu all over the world.

Yoga is another ancient exercise. It is also common today. Yoga was invented in India. It involves stretching, movement, and breathing exercises. There is **evidence** that people were practicing yoga at least 5,000 years ago. Ancient stones from 3000 BCE **include** carvings of people in yoga poses. However, many people believe that yoga didn't start in 3000 BCE. They think it began much earlier than that.

Exercise and physical fitness were extremely important in ancient Greece. The ancient Greeks probably cared more about exercise than any other group of people. They thought that exercising the body was as important as exercising the mind. Therefore, they made exercise a big part of their society. Some of the types of exercise that the Greeks enjoyed included gymnastics, running, jumping, and wrestling—a type of fighting. The ancient Greeks created the Olympic Games in 776 BCE. For almost 12 centuries, athletes competed in the Games every four years. Today, countries all over the globe compete in the Olympic Games.

Physical fitness has been a part of human history for thousands of years. Exercises and events that began far in the past continue today. Do you think that exercises and events from today will be popular thousands of years from now?

Stop and Think

Why do you think no one really knows when people started exercising?

Check Your Understanding

B. Write three examples of exercise in the past.

1. _____

2. _____

3. _____

GO ONLINE
for more
practice

GO ONLINE
for more
practice

Vocabulary Strategy

Descriptive Adjectives

Descriptive adjectives give more information about nouns. They usually describe things like feelings, taste, appearance, size, color, and shape. Learning descriptive adjectives will help you understand the details the writer includes. Look at the examples.

*Sarah is **nervous**.*   *I feel **calm**.*   *The soup is **hot**.*

C. Read each set of words. Circle the word that is NOT a descriptive adjective.

1. exciting	(example)	convenient	social
2. rude	enjoyable	successful	game
3. exercise	healthy	interesting	happy
4. sad	large	round	enjoy
5. modern	play	great	angry

D. Look at the words you circled in Activity C. What part of speech is each word? Write the word and the part of speech.

1. _____example_____ _____noun_____   2. _____ _____

3. _____ _____   4. _____ _____

5 _____ _____

Reading Strategy

Identify Cause and Effect

A *cause* is the reason that something happened. An *effect* is the thing that happened. Writers use certain words to describe cause and effect relationships. Understanding these words will help you identify the causes and effects when you read. Here are some examples.

to describe a cause: *because*   *because of*
to describe an effect: *as a result*   *therefore*   *so*

E. Look at the text on page 62. Find and underline an example of each word or phrase. Then write the cause and effect.

1. because   cause: _____

                effect: _____

2. so   cause: _____

                effect: _____

3. therefore   cause: _____

                effect: _____

◉ Reading 2

A. Listen and read along.

What Are the Effects of Exercise?

You probably already know that exercise can help you lose weight and stay fit. However, it has a lot of other good **effects**, too. Are you healthy and fit? Even if you are, there are several reasons that you should exercise.

First, exercise can give you **energy**. When you are tired during the day and you can't study or work, don't take a nap. Take a walk or go for a run instead. Researchers looked at 70 different studies about exercise and fatigue— extreme tiredness. In the studies, people who didn't exercise started to exercise

regularly. As a result, they felt less fatigue. They didn't feel tired during the day. Over 90 percent of the studies showed the same results: regular exercise increased energy and reduced fatigue.

Second, exercise can help you sleep better. It's important to get enough sleep. Lack of sleep is one of the main **causes** of stress. Exercising raises your body temperature. Your temperature goes back to normal about five to six hours after you exercise. You become sleepy at this point because the drop in temperature tells your body that it's time to sleep.

Also, exercise can reduce stress and anxiety. Do you ever feel **nervous** or

stressed? Working out for 20 minutes can make you feel **calm**. How? When you exercise, you have to focus on your body, so you can't think about your stressful thoughts. In addition, when you exercise, your body creates a special chemical. This chemical can help your brain react to stress.

Finally, studies show that exercise is good for your brain, especially your memory. Exercising makes your body create new cells in a part of the brain called the hippocampus. Memory and learning happen in the hippocampus. Because of this increase in cells, exercising can improve your memory and make it easier to learn new things.

Regular exercise can improve your life in so many ways. It can make you feel better, look better, and do more. So why are you sitting there reading? Go out and exercise!

Grammar in the Readings

Notice irregular past tense verbs in the readings.

Some verbs are irregular in the simple past tense. You have to memorize these forms.

begin → began   *go → went*   *feel → felt*
make → made   *take → took*   *think → thought*

*People **began** exercising thousands of years ago.*
*They **thought** exercise was important.*

Irregular past tense verbs stay the same for all subjects.

*I **took** a nap.*   *She **took** a nap.*   *They **took** naps.*

GO ONLINE
for grammar practice

Check Your Understanding

B. Write four effects of exercise.

Effect 1
_____
_____
_____

Effect 2
_____
_____
_____

Effects of Exercise

Effect 3
_____
_____
_____

Effect 4
_____
_____
_____

Vocabulary Strategy: Descriptive Adjectives

C. Complete the sentences with the words from the box.

calm	fit	nervous	stressed	tired

1. Most people exercise because they want to be healthy and _____fit_____.

2. If you are _____ during the day, don't take a nap. Take a walk.

3. Work and school can make you feel _____ and

   _____. Exercise can make you _____.

Reading Strategy: Identify Cause and Effect

D. Look at the text on page 64. Find and underline an example for each statement or phrase. Then write the cause and effect.

1. as a result

cause: _____

effect: _____

2. because

cause: _____

effect: _____

3. because of

cause: _____

effect: _____

4. so

cause: _____

effect: _____

● Make Connections: Text to Text

A. Read each sentence. Does it describe Reading 1, Reading 2, or both? Write the letter of each sentence in the Venn diagram.

a. Five to six hours after you exercise, you might feel sleepy.

b. If you feel stressed, you should exercise.

c. Exercise was a big part of life in ancient Greece.

d. People in ancient China thought that exercise was important.

e. Exercising regularly can improve your memory.

f. One reason people exercise is to feel healthy.

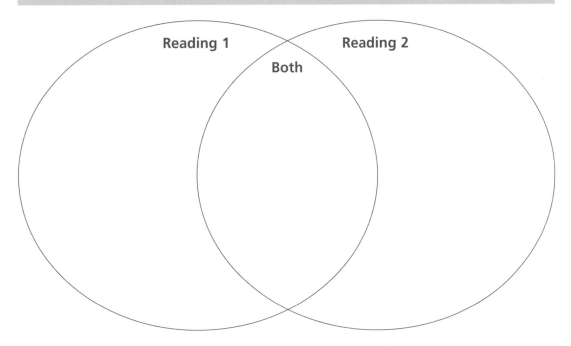

B. Complete each sentence with information from the readings. Different answers are possible.

1. People in ancient Greece probably created the Olympic Games because they wanted to

_____

_____

2. People in ancient China probably invented kung fu because they wanted to

_____

_____

3. People in ancient India created yoga. Therefore, they probably knew that

_____

_____

Summarizing and Retelling

A. Complete the sentences with the words from the box. Then read the sentences to a partner to summarize.

Nouns	Verbs	Adjectives
cause effects energy evidence	include	ancient calm fit modern nervous

1. There is _____ that people have been exercising for thousands of years.

2. For example, a(n) _____ stone tablet from 3000 BCE shows people doing yoga.

3. Types of sports _____ swimming, soccer, and golf.

4. Kung fu is an old sport that is still popular in _____ times.

5. Exercising has a lot of good _____.

6. First, it makes us healthy and _____.

7. If we're stressed or _____, exercising for 20 minutes can make us

   feel _____.

8. Not getting enough sleep can be a(n) _____ of stress. Exercise can reduce stress.

9. If you feel tired, exercise can give you more _____.

B. Answer the questions with a partner.

1. There is evidence that people started exercising thousands of years ago. Think about the country you live in. Do you think people there two hundred years ago exercised as much as people today? Why or why not?

2. What do you think is the most important effect of exercise for you? Explain.

Word Partners

take a nap

take a walk

take medicine

take a break

take some time off

_____

GO ONLINE
to practice
word partners

● Make Connections: Text to World

A. Answer the questions.

1. Do you think people today exercise enough? Too much? Explain.

_____

_____

_____

2. Imagine that it is the year 4000. What kinds of evidence do you think people will find that show that we used to exercise?

_____

_____

_____

3. What are some reasons that companies should give employees time to exercise during the day? Explain.

_____

_____

_____

4. What are some other ways to:

reduce stress and anxiety?

_____

_____

increase your energy?

_____

_____

improve your sleep?

_____

_____

improve your memory?

_____

_____

B. Talk about your answers from Activity A with a partner. Look at the Oxford 2000 keywords on page 133 and find five words to help you.

Chant

GO ONLINE
for the
Chapter 4
Vocabulary &
Grammar Chant

CHAPTER 5

What Can We Learn from the Past?

- /ɛ/ sound
- Word families
- Contrast signal words
- Past progressive; adjective + infinitive

▲ BEFORE READING ▶ Oxford 2000 🔑 words to talk about life in the past

Learn Vocabulary

A. Match each picture to the correct description.

__1__ A **chemical** is a substance made with chemistry.

This diet soda is full of chemicals. It's not natural.

_____ If something is **average**, it's normal or typical.

On an average day, it's sunny and warm.

_____ **Pollution** is the act of making the air and water dirty and dangerous.

Cars cause a lot of pollution.

_____ A **disease** is a serious illness.

Scientists create new medicines to fight diseases.

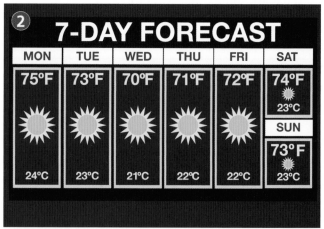

B. Match each description to the correct picture.

1. A **variety** is a lot of different things.

   I bought a variety of foods at the supermarket.

2. If something is **natural**, it was not made by people.

   The soup has all natural ingredients.

3. If something is **available**, people can have it.

   If you need a job, go to the shoe store. There are jobs available.

4. There are four **seasons** in a year—spring, summer, winter, and fall.

   Spring is my favorite season because I like to see the flowers bloom.

5. When something is **convenient**, it makes your life easier.

   I can stop for a drink without leaving my car. It's so convenient.

6. A **century** is a period of 100 years.

   My grandfather turned 100 today. He's one century old!

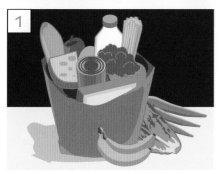

C. Complete the paragraph with the words from the box. You won't use two of the words.

Oxford 2000 🔑

Use the Oxford 2000 list on page 133 to find more words to describe the pictures on these pages. Share your words with a partner.

~~century~~	convenient	natural	seasons
chemicals	diseases	pollution	

Today, most factories try to keep the air and water clean. A _____century_____ ago,

people didn't really think about _____—they didn't try to keep the earth

clean. Factories put _____ in the water. Smoke from factories made the air

hard to breathe. Dirty air and water can cause _____, so people in big cities

often got sick. Now we try harder to protect the _____ environment. We

realize that we need to protect the oceans, rivers, lakes, and forests.

GO ONLINE
for more
practice

Preview the Text

D. Look at the picture on page 74. Write a short answer to each question.

1. What do you see in the big picture?

_____

2. Which of these foods do you like?

_____

3. Which do you not like? Why don't you like them?

_____

E. Look at the text on page 74. Write a short answer to each question.

1. What is the title?

_____

2. What do you think the answer to the title question is? Why?

_____

_____

3. What kinds of food do you think people ate 100 years ago?

_____

Sounds of English

Spelling Connection

🔊 A. Listen to the word *health*. What sound does the *ea* make? The sound /ɛ/ can be spelled with *ea* or *e*. Circle four words below that have the same sound as in *health*. Listen for /ɛ/.

| *better* | *fresh* | *meat* | *easy* | *yes* | *sell* |

🔊 B. Listen to the words. Circle the vocabulary words with the same sound as in *health*.

| chemical | natural | century | season | average |

⬤ Make Connections: Text to Self

A. Answer the questions.

1. Where do you shop for food?

_____

2. Do you think you have healthy or unhealthy eating habits? Explain.

_____

3. What do you eat and drink in an average week? List as many foods and drinks as you can.

_____

_____

_____

_____

4. What kinds of food do you think people ate on an average day 100 years ago?

_____

_____

B. Look at your answer to question 3 in Activity A. Write each food item in the correct column. Then compare your answer to question 2 with your chart. In general, do you eat healthy foods or unhealthy foods?

Healthy Foods	Unhealthy Foods

◉) **Reading 1**

A. Read the text on your own.

Did People Eat Healthier in the Past?

frozen food

In most places in the world today, it is easy to find healthy food. With supermarkets, buying healthy food like fresh fruits, vegetables, fish, and meat is easy and **convenient**. However, it is also easy to find unhealthy food today. Supermarkets and other stores sell good food, but they also sell frozen foods and junk food like chips, candy, and cookies. A lot of food today contains **chemicals**. Research has shown that many of these chemicals are bad for our health. So did people in the past eat healthier than we do today?

A **century** ago, people didn't eat junk food or frozen food. Instead, they ate **natural** foods without chemicals. On the other hand, their natural foods were not always as good as food today. In the past, meat often came from sick animals. It's not healthy to eat meat from a sick animal. In most places today, laws make sure that food is safe.

J&J Supermarket

Stop and Think

How do you think people shopped for food 100 years ago?

junk food: chips, candy, and cookies

In most countries today, we can buy a **variety** of foods. We can buy oranges in the winter and apples in the summer. Healthy fruits and vegetables are **available** at any time of year. These foods come from all over the world. In the past, this kind of variety was not possible. People could eat certain foods only in certain **seasons**.

We eat much more meat, sugar, fattening foods, and chemicals today than people did a century ago. Studies show that these things can cause heart **disease** and a variety of other health problems. However, people live much longer now. Today, the **average** person lives for 70 to 80 years. In contrast, 100 years ago, the average person lived for only about 50 years. People live longer because we have better medicine now. But people also have longer lives because healthy food is almost always available.

So did people eat healthier in the past? Yes and no. People in the past did eat more natural food than we do now. But, in some ways, we also eat better today. We *can* eat healthier today than people did in the past. We just have to *choose* to eat good foods.

B. Content words, such as nouns, verbs, and adjectives, receive more stress than function words. Listen to the first paragraph of the reading on page 74 and underline the content words.

Check Your Understanding

C. Find evidence in the reading on page 74 to support each statement in the chart.

People Ate Healthier in the Past	People Eat Healthier Now

Vocabulary Strategy

Word Families
Word families are groups of words that have the same base word. The words in word families are usually different parts of speech. Learning word families instead of single words can help you learn a large amount of vocabulary quickly. Look at the examples.

noun: *safety*   adjective: *safe*   adverb: *safely*

GO ONLINE for more practice

D. Complete the chart.

Nouns	Verbs	Adjectives	Adverbs
nature		natural	naturally
_____	vary	various	variously
convenience		_____	conveniently
availability	avail	_____	
choice	_____	chosen	

Reading Strategy

Contrast Signal Words
Writers use certain words and phrases to contrast two things or talk about how they are different. Learning how something is different from another thing can help you understand it better. Here are some examples of words that signal contrast.

but   however   instead   on the other hand   in contrast

GO ONLINE for more practice

E. Look at the text on page 74. Find and underline an example of each word or phrase. Then write the two contrasted things.

1. but

_____

_____

2. however

_____

_____

3. instead

_____

_____

4. on the other hand

_____

_____

5. in contrast

_____

_____

◉ Reading 2

A. Listen and read along.

How Did People in the Past Produce Energy?

Stop and Think

Before you read the second paragraph, what do you think three of the oldest sources of power are?

There are about 7 billion people on Earth today, and we use a lot of energy. In most places today, people use natural gas or oil to make energy. In some places, people have started to use energy from wind and from the sun. But what did people use in the past? Humans used several different things to make energy.

The first energy source was probably wood. Wood was easy to find and easy to use. Early humans used wood to stay warm and to cook food. We don't know when early humans learned how to make fire. However, we know that people were burning wood for energy at least 1 million years ago. In some areas of the world, wood is still an important and **convenient** source of energy.

One of the oldest energy sources is coal. Coal looks like rock, but it is made of very old plants. Thousands of years ago, people were burning coal for heat and energy. During the 1800s, coal became a very important source of energy. People used it to power ships, trains, and factories. People all over the world still use coal today because there is a lot of it underground. However, burning coal causes a lot of air **pollution**.

Coal can be burned for heat and energy.

Water is another very old source of energy. There is evidence that the ancient Greeks were using water for energy over 2,000 years ago. How? They built big wheels out of wood. Then they put part of a wheel underwater, such as in a river. The moving water caused the wheel to turn and make energy. We still use water for energy today, but the wheels today are much larger. We call this kind of energy "hydropower." The prefix "hydro" means water.

We have used wood, coal, and water power for a very long time. Water is a renewable source of energy. We won't run out of it. In contrast, wood and coal are not renewable. Sun, wind, and water power are becoming more **available** around the world. What do you think will be the most popular source of power in the future?

water wheel

Grammar in the Readings

Notice the past progressive in the reading.

Writers often use the past progressive to give background information in a story. To form the past progressive, use *was* or *were* with verb + *-ing*.

*People **were burning** wood for energy at least 1 million years ago.*

Notice adjective + infinitive in the reading.

Writers often use *it* + *is/was* (*not*) + adjective + infinitive to give an opinion about an activity.

*Wood was a good choice for energy. It was **easy to find**.*

To connect the idea to a person or people, add *for* + noun after the adjective.

*It was **easy for people** to find wood.*

GO ONLINE
for grammar practice

Check Your Understanding

B. Complete the chart with information from the reading.

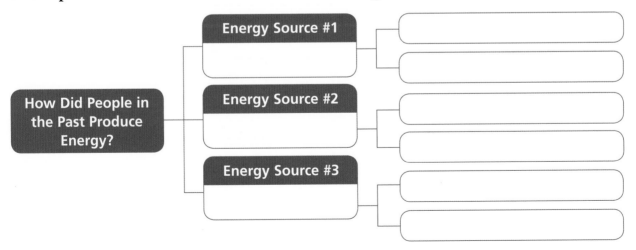

Vocabulary Strategy: Word Families

C. Complete the chart with the words from the box. Use a dictionary for help.

energetic	ease	power	polluted	popularly
~~energize~~	easily	powerfully	popularize	
energetically	powerful	pollute	popularity	

Nouns	Verbs	Adjectives	Adverbs
energy	_energize_	_____	_____
_____		easy	_____
power	_____	_____	_____
pollution	_____	_____	
_____	_____	popular	_____

Reading Strategy: Contrast Signal Words

D. Look at the text on pages 76–77. Find and underline an example of each word or phrase. Then write the two contrasted things.

1. however

_____

_____

2. but (paragraph 1)

_____

_____

3. but (paragraph 3)

_____

_____

4. but (paragraph 4)

_____

_____

5. in contrast

_____

_____

◖● Make Connections: Text to Text

A. Read each sentence. Does it describe Reading 1, Reading 2, or both? Write the letter of each sentence in the Venn diagram.

a. A hundred years ago, people ate natural food.

b. We have used coal for power for thousands of years.

c. Water turns wheels to create power.

d. People burned wood to cook food at least 1 million years ago.

e. These days, a bigger variety of fruits and vegetables is available.

f. Life in the past was different in some ways and the same in other ways.

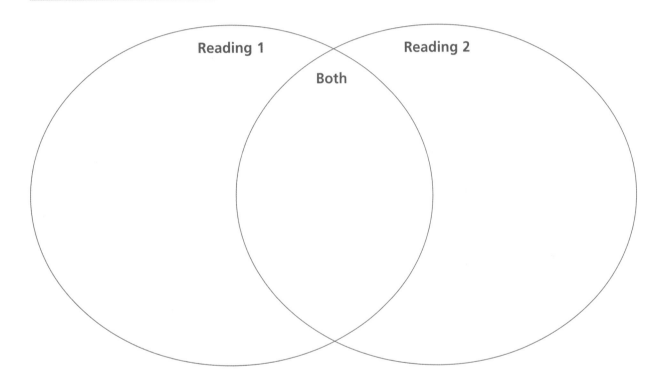

B. Complete each sentence with information from the readings and your own ideas. Different answers are possible.

1. Two hundred years ago, people probably ate _____ for dinner and used _____ power to cook their food.

2. Two hundred years from now, people will probably eat _____ for dinner and use _____ power to cook their food.

3. I think people in the past (were healthier / were not healthier) than we are now because

_____

Summarizing and Retelling

A. Complete the sentences with the words from the box. Then read the sentences to a partner to summarize.

Nouns	Adjectives
century	available
chemicals	average
disease	convenient
pollution	natural
season	
variety	

1. A(n) _____ ago, people could only buy _____ foods like fruits, vegetables, and meat.

2. Food in the past didn't have _____ in it.

3. These days, we can buy a(n) _____ of foods at any time of the year.

4. All kinds of fruits and vegetables are _____ at any time of the year.

5. We don't have to wait for a certain _____ to buy certain foods.

6. Supermarkets also sell _____ foods, such as frozen dinners.

7. When people don't eat well, they aren't healthy. It's easy to get a(n) _____ when you don't eat well.

8. People live a lot longer now than they did in the past. Today, the _____ person lives for 70 to 80 years.

9. Some types of energy sources cause _____ . For example, coal can make the air dirty and hard to breathe.

B. Answer the questions with a partner.

1. How do you think shopping for food and cooking was more difficult 300 years ago? How do you think it was easier?

2. Do you think you would like to live in the past? Why or why not?

Word Partners

baby food

fast food

fresh food

frozen food

healthy food

junk food

pet food

GO ONLINE
to practice
word partners

◐ Make Connections: Text to World

A. Answer the questions.

1. Do you think people today care about healthy food? Explain.

_____

_____

_____

2. Imagine that you lived 100 years ago. Describe a typical day in your life. Focus on food and energy.

_____

_____

_____

3. According to Reading 1, fresh fruits and vegetables are more available now. How do you think this affects people's health? List three or four ways.

_____

_____

_____

4. Think about how people produced energy 100 years ago. In what ways is energy production better for the Earth now?

_____

_____

_____

B. Talk about your answers to Activity A with a partner. Look at the Oxford 2000 keywords on page 133 and find five words to help you.

Chant

GO ONLINE
for the
Chapter 5
Vocabulary &
Grammar Chant

CHAPTER **6** Food Innovation

- Final /s/, /z/, and /ɪz/ sounds
- Comparative adjectives
- Sequence events
- *used to* + verb

▲ **BEFORE READING** ▶ Oxford 2000 🔑 words to talk about food history

Learn Vocabulary

A. Match each picture to the correct description.

_____ A **restaurant** is a place where you can buy and eat cooked food.

Antonio's Pizza is my favorite restaurant.

__1__ A **meal** is food that you eat at a certain time, such as the morning, afternoon, or evening.

I eat three meals a day: breakfast, lunch, and dinner.

_____ If you **serve** food or drinks to someone, you give them food or drinks.

I serve food at Antonio's Pizza.

_____ If you **deliver** something, you take it to the person who wants it.

I deliver food for Antonio's Pizza.

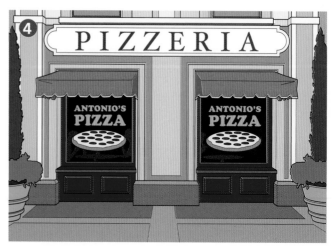

B. Match each description to the correct picture.

1. If you **keep** something a certain condition, you make it stay the same condition.

   This bag keeps drinks cold.

2. A **method** is a way of doing something.

   Do you know a good method for cleaning pots and pans?

3. If a frozen thing **melts**, it becomes soft or liquid.

   Eat your ice cream. It's melting!

4. If you **store** something, you put it away, so you can use it in the future.

   I store my sugar and flour in glass jars.

5. If you **collect** something, you bring a large amount of it together.

   I'm collecting money for my school. We need new books.

6. If food or drink **spoils**, it is not good to eat or drink anymore.

   Milk spoils after two or three weeks.

C. Complete the conversation with the words from the box. You won't use two of the words.

Oxford 2000 🔑

Use the Oxford 2000 list on page 133 to find more words to describe the pictures on these pages. Share your words with a partner.

delivers	meals	~~restaurant~~	spoiled
keep	melted	serve	store

A: Do you want to go out for dinner? There's a great Italian ___restaurant___ down the street. They _____ really good pizza there.

B: I don't think I want to go out. Let's cook something.

A: I don't have any food. My refrigerator broke last week. All the food _____, and all the ice _____.

B: Oh, no! I'm sorry. Where do you eat?

A: I eat all my _____ at restaurants. I'm going to get a new refrigerator this weekend.

B: Well, the restaurant _____ food. I will call and order a pizza.

GO ONLINE for more practice

Preview the Text

D. Look at the pictures on page 86. Write a short answer to each question.

1. What do you see in the pictures?

_____

2. Why do you think these pictures are included?

_____

E. Look at the text on page 86. Write a short answer to each question.

1. What is the title? _____

2. What do you think the answer to the title question is? Why?

_____

_____

3. What are the coolest seasons of the year? The warmest?

_____

_____

Sounds of English

Spelling Connection

🔊 A. Remember that there are three possible ending sounds for plural *s* and third person singular *s*: /s/, /z/, and /ɪz/. We say the /z/ sound after the voiced sounds like /b/, /g/, /l/, /r/, /w/, /v/, /m/, /n/, /y/, and all vowels. We say the /s/ sound after the voiceless sounds like /p/, /k/, /t/, and /f/. We say the /ɪz/ sound after /s/, /z/, /tʃ/, and /dʒ/ sounds. Listen to the examples.

	/s/	/z/	/ɪz/
verbs:	*keeps*	*spoils*	*watches*
nouns:	*fruits*	*methods*	*houses*

🔊 B. Listen to the plural nouns and third person singular verbs. Circle the ending sound that you hear.

1. centuries   a. /s/   (b. /z/)   c. /ɪz/

2. places   a. /s/   b. /z/   c. /ɪz/

3. cooks   a. /s/   b. /z/   c. /ɪz/

4. drinks   a. /s/   b. /z/   c. /ɪz/

5. melts   a. /s/   b. /z/   c. /ɪz/

◐ Make Connections: Text to Self

A. Answer the questions.

1. What kinds of things do you put in a refrigerator? List as many foods and drinks as you can.

_____

_____

_____

2. Food has to stay cool. What other things have to stay cool? List as many ideas as you can.

_____

_____

_____

3. What kinds of things do you think people had to keep cool 100 years ago?

_____

_____

B. What are some foods that have to go in the refrigerator? What are some foods that should not go in the refrigerator? What are some foods that can go in the refrigerator but don't have to stay cool? Write each food item in the correct place in the Venn diagram.

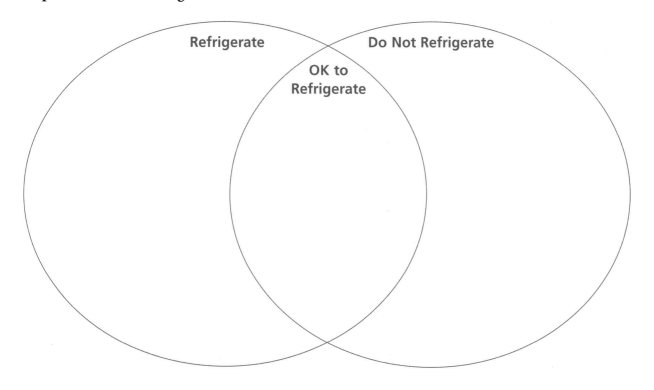

▲▲ DURING READING
▶ Vocabulary strategy: Comparative adjectives
▶ Reading strategy: Sequence events

◉ Reading 1

A. When we read numbers for centuries, for example, *1500s*, we say *fifteen hundreds*. Underline two examples of centuries in the reading.

B. Now read the text on your own.

How Did We Keep Things Cool?

Stop and Think

Why is it important to keep some food cool?

a stream

a cave

digging a hole

sawdust

What do you do when you want a cold drink? You probably get a drink from your refrigerator. Or you get ice from your freezer to make your drink cold. But people did not have refrigerators before the early 1900s. How did they **keep** things cool before then?

In the past, it was difficult to keep food cold. Warm food **spoils** quickly. Before refrigerators were available, people used to get sick a lot or even die from eating spoiled food. In the past, people tried many different **methods** to keep things cold. They used to put food in cool streams or in caves near their homes. They also **stored** food like vegetables and fruits in rooms under their houses. These rooms stayed cooler in warm months. However, none of these methods was perfect.

What was a better way? Putting food on ice. In 1000 BCE, people in China **collected** ice and snow. Then they dug holes under their homes and filled them with the ice and snow. After that, they put their food in the holes. In many countries, people continued to do this for about 2,000 years.

There are a few problems with this method. First, ice and snow are not available everywhere. Second, ice **melts**. An American businessman named Frederick Tudor solved these problems. He wanted to **deliver** ice to hot places, such as the Caribbean. In the early 1800s, he sent a ship full of ice from Boston, Massachusetts, to the island of Martinique. Almost all of the ice melted. After that happened, Tudor realized that he had to find a way to keep the ice frozen. He spent ten years working on the problem. Eventually, he tried putting sawdust—very small pieces of wood—between the pieces of ice. It worked! Sawdust keeps ice frozen for a longer period of time.

People used to work hard to keep their food and drinks cold. Now, it's much easier. The next time you want a cold drink, imagine your life without a refrigerator.

Check Your Understanding

C. Complete the statements with information from the reading on page 86.

1. In the past, people sometimes put food under their _____houses_____ to keep the food cool.

2. They also sometimes put food in _____ and _____.

3. In ancient China, people put their food on _____ and _____.

4. One problem with using ice is it's not _____ everywhere.

5. Another problem is that it _____ when it's warm outside.

6. Frederick Tudor wanted to _____ ice to people.

7. He discovered that ice could stay frozen if he put _____ between pieces of ice.

Vocabulary Strategy

Comparative Adjectives

We use comparative adjectives to compare two nouns. Learning comparative adjectives will help you understand comparisons writers make. For adjectives with one or two syllables, we usually add *-er* to the end of the word. Sometimes, the spelling of the word changes.

big → bigger   *busy → busier*

For adjectives with three or more syllables, we usually add the word *more* before the adjective.

*Brazil is a big country. China is **bigger**.*
*Food from a restaurant is convenient. Frozen food is **more convenient**.*

Some adjectives have irregular comparative forms.

good → better   *bad → worse*

GO ONLINE
for more
practice

D. Complete the chart with comparative forms of the adjectives. Use a dictionary for correct spelling if necessary.

Adjective	Comparative	Adjective	Comparative
long	_____	cool	_____
good	_____	easy	_____

GO ONLINE
for more
practice

Sequence Events

Writers use certain words and phrases to show the sequence, or order, in which things happened. Sequence words help you figure out the order of events in the texts you read.

in the past	before	in (+ a year or period of time)	later
then	after that	first	second	eventually	now

E. Look at the text on page 86. Find and underline an example of each word or phrase. Then write the sentence that the word or phrase appears in.

1. in the past

In the past, it was difficult to keep food cold.

2. before

3. in (+ a year or period of time)

4. then

5. after that

6. eventually

7. now

◉ Reading 2

A. Listen and read along.

A Short History of the Restaurant

Stop and Think

Before you read the second paragraph, what is one way that you think restaurants in the past were different from today's restaurants?

Do you know when **restaurants** were invented? The first restaurants were invented thousands of years ago. However, they were very different from restaurants today.

The first restaurants were in ancient Greece and ancient Rome. These restaurants **served** food in large stone bowls. People didn't order food from a menu. Everyone used to share the food from big bowls. People believe that these places were very popular because most homes in ancient Greece and Rome did not have kitchens. Also, people didn't have to **store** food at home if they ate their **meals** at these restaurants.

Later, restaurants began to open in China. In the early 1100s, more than 1 million people lived in the city of Hangzhou, China. It was a very busy city, and people had money. All of these people had to eat. Smart cooks started cooking and selling food along the Imperial Way, a very big street in the city. Unlike in ancient Greece and Rome, people in China could choose food from a menu. They didn't have to eat the same food as everyone else.

For the next several centuries, there were restaurants all over the world. People could buy food on the street or at inns—small

a restaurant in ancient Greece

hotels. Then, in the middle of the 1700s, restaurants started opening in Paris. These restaurants were more similar to restaurants we know today. There was a bigger variety of food, and eating in these restaurants was a more enjoyable experience. In the 19th century, trains made travel much faster and simpler. Eventually, this type of restaurant began to appear all over Europe and in other parts of the world.

Now, restaurants are everywhere. You can buy a variety of different types of food. You can have food delivered to your door. But remember it wasn't always like that.

Grammar in the Readings

Notice *used to* + verb in the readings.

You can use *used to* with a verb to say that something was true in the past but is not true now.

*In the past, people **used to** put food in caves to keep it cool.*
*Everyone **used to** share the food from big bowls.*
*We **used to** play baseball when we were kids.*

GO ONLINE for grammar practice

Check Your Understanding

B. Answer the questions with information from the reading.

1. Where were the first restaurants?

Greece and Rome

2. What is one way that these restaurants were different from today's restaurants?

3. Why were these restaurants popular?

4. When did the first restaurants open in China?

_____

5. What is one way restaurants in China were different from the first restaurants?

_____

6. Where and when did restaurants more similar to today's restaurants open?

_____

Recycle

the Vocabulary
Strategy

Vocabulary Strategy: Comparative Adjectives

C. Complete the chart with comparative forms of the adjectives. Use a dictionary for correct spelling if necessary.

Adjective	Comparative	Adjective	Comparative
fast	_____	similar	_____
enjoyable	_____	big	_____
simple	_____	warm	_____

Recycle

the Reading
Strategy

Reading Strategy: Sequence Events

D. Look at the text on pages 88–89. Find and underline an example of each word or phrase. Then write the sentence that the word or phrase appears in.

1. first

_____

2. later

_____

3. then

_____

4. in (+ a year or period of time)

_____

5. eventually

_____

● Make Connections: Text to Text

A. Read each sentence. Does it describe Reading 1, Reading 2, or both? Write the letter of each sentence in the Venn diagram.

a. Restaurants in ancient Greece were different from restaurants today.

b. Two hundred years ago, restaurants in Paris were similar to restaurants now.

c. It's easy to keep food cool these days.

d. People used to collect ice and snow to keep their food cool.

e. Kitchens have changed a lot since ancient times.

f. People began selling food in China around 1000 BCE.

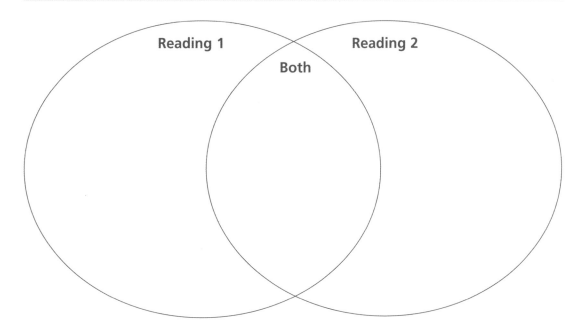

B. Complete each sentence with information from the readings. Different answers are possible.

1. How is a restaurant convenient for people who don't have refrigerators?

_____

_____

2. In Paris in the 1800s, restaurants didn't have refrigerators. How do you think they kept their food cool?

_____

_____

3. Do you think the invention of refrigerators made restaurants more popular or not as popular? Explain.

_____

_____

Summarizing and Retelling

A. Complete the sentences with the words from the box. Some of the words have to be changed to fit the sentences. For example, *restaurant* has to be changed to *restaurants*. Then read the sentences to a partner to summarize.

Nouns	Verbs
meal	collect
method	deliver
restaurant	keep
	melt
	serve
	spoil
	store

1. In the past, it wasn't easy to _____ food cold.

2. If food wasn't cold, it could _____ quickly.

3. Some people used to _____ snow and ice and _____ their food on them.

4. But that wasn't a perfect _____ because snow and ice _____ in warm weather.

5. The first _____ were in ancient Rome and ancient Greece.

6. Those restaurants _____ food in large stone bowls.

7. A lot of people ate their _____ in those places because they didn't have kitchens.

8. Now there are restaurants everywhere. Some restaurants _____ food to people's homes.

B. Answer the questions with a partner.

1. What is the most surprising thing you learned about the history of keeping things cool? The history of restaurants?

2. How do you think restaurants of the future will be different from today's restaurants?

Word Partners

keep (something) cold

keep (someone or something) safe

keep a promise

keep a secret

keep in touch

keep calm

keep an appointment

GO ONLINE
to practice word partners

⬤ Make Connections: Text to World

A. Answer the questions.

1. Imagine that we suddenly don't have refrigerators. How is your life different?

_____

_____

2. Imagine that there are no restaurants near you. Is this a problem for you or not? Explain.

_____

_____

3. What is your favorite restaurant? Why do you like it?

_____

_____

4. Which do you like more: eating at home or eating in a restaurant? Why?

_____

_____

B. Talk about your answer to question 4 in Activity A with a partner and complete the chart with as many ideas as you can. Look at the Oxford 2000 keywords on page 133 and find five words to help you.

Benefits of Eating at Home	Benefits of Eating in a Restaurant

Chant

GO ONLINE for the Chapter 6 Vocabulary & Grammar Chant

Extend Your Skills

Look at the word bank for Unit 2. Check (✓) the words you know. Circle the words you want to learn better.

OXFORD 2000 🔑		
Adjectives	**Nouns**	**Verbs**
ancient	century	cause
available	chemical	collect
average	disease	deliver
calm	effect	include
convenient	energy	keep
fit	evidence	melt
modern	meal	serve
natural	method	spoil
nervous	pollution	store
	restaurant	
	season	
	variety	

PRACTICE WITH THE OXFORD 2000 🔑

A. Use the words in the chart. Match adjectives with nouns.

1. _____ancient evidence_____   2. _____

3. _____   4. _____

5. _____

B. Use the words in the chart. Match verbs with nouns.

1. _____cause disease_____   2. _____

3. _____   4. _____

5. _____

C. Use the words in the chart. Match verbs with adjective noun partners.

1. _____store available energy_____   2. _____

3. _____   4. _____

5. _____

UNIT 3 Future

CHAPTER **7** Cities of the Future

- Voiceless and voiced th /θ/ sounds
- Collocations with *take*
- Scan for information
- *more/less* + noun; *will* + verb

▲ BEFORE READING ► Oxford 2000 ✎ words to talk about cities

Learn Vocabulary

A. Match each description to the correct picture.

1. **International** means between countries.

   I have a very international group of friends. They come from all over the world.

2. If something **grows**, it gets bigger.

   Tommy is growing fast. I have to buy new pants for him.

3. If one thing **affects** another thing, it causes the second thing to change in a specific way.

   Some lotions affect my skin. They give me a rash.

4. If two or more people or things **connect**, they are joined.

   I can go online. My computer is connected to the Internet.

5. A **center** of something is a place where that thing happens a lot.

   Many people think of Paris as a center of fashion.

6. **Twice** means two times.

   I have been to Mexico City twice—once in 2010 and once in 2014.

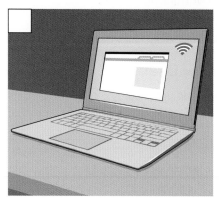

B. Match each picture to the correct description.

_____ **Business** is the buying and selling of things to make money.

The business center is in the city.

_____ If someone is an **expert**, he or she has special knowledge or skills.

My uncle is an art expert. He explains art to other people.

1 A city or country's **economy** is the way it spends money and makes, buys, and sells things.

Our economy is strong right now. It is growing.

_____ Something **financial** is connected to money.

Many financial organizations work with money.

C. Complete the paragraph with the words from the box. You won't use two of the words.

Oxford 2000 🗝

Use the Oxford 2000 list on page 133 to find more words to describe the pictures on these pages. Share your words with a partner.

affect	centers	economy	financial	international
business	connected	experts	~~growing~~	twice

Our company is _____growing_____ very quickly. We opened two _____

offices last month. One is in Barcelona, and the other one is in London. We are very excited

about that office because London is one of the most important _____

_____. There are a lot of important banks in London. I've gone to London

_____ in the past year. While I was there, I _____ with

several financial _____. I discussed our plans for our _____

with them. They gave me a lot of useful tips. I will discuss these tips at our next meeting.

GO ONLINE for more practice

Preview the Text

D. Look at the text on page 100. Answer the questions.

1. What is the title?

_____

2. What do you think the answer to the title question is? Why?

_____

_____

3. How many people do you think there are in the world today?

_____

4. How many people do you think there will be in the year 2050?

_____

Sounds of English

Spelling Connection

A. The letters *th* are usually pronounced in one of two ways: voiceless or voiced. To pronounce voiceless th /θ/, put your tongue between your teeth and release air from your mouth. To pronounce voiced th /ð/, do the same thing, but this time, make your vocal cords vibrate.

voiceless th /θ/: *think   with*   voiced th /ð/: *this   breathe*

B. Listen to the words. Circle the *th* sound that you hear.

1. third   a. voiceless th   b. voiced th
2. there   a. voiceless th   b. voiced th
3. this   a. voiceless th   b. voiced th
4. thing   a. voiceless th   b. voiced th
5. they   a. voiceless th   b. voiced th

● Make Connections: Text to Self

A. Answer the questions.

1. Do you think your city is growing quickly? Why or why not?

_____

_____

_____

2. What are some good things about living in a big city?

_____

_____

_____

_____

3. What are some good things about living in a small city?

_____

_____

_____

_____

B. Which do you think is better: living in a big city or living in a small city? Complete the chart. Then decide if you want to live in a big city or a small city.

	Big Cities	Small Cities
Good Things		
Bad Things		

◉ Reading 1

A. Read the text on your own.

What Areas of the World Are Growing the Fastest?

Two hundred years ago, there were about 1 billion people in the world. One hundred years ago, there were about 1.8 billion people. Today, there are about 7 billion people on Earth. The population—the number of people in the world—has **grown** very quickly over the past 100 years, and it continues to grow. What parts of the world have grown the fastest?

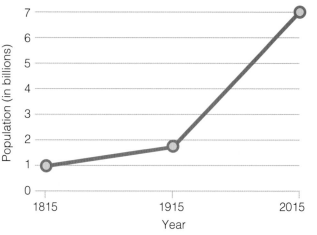

Stop and Think

Why do you think the population is growing faster now?

Researchers say that developing countries are growing the fastest. Developing countries are countries without a lot of money. Many of the fastest-growing countries in the world are in Africa. Right now, there are about 1.1 billion people in Africa. **Experts** believe that Africa will have **twice** as many people by 2050.

Africa's population is growing the fastest, but Asia still has more people than any other part of the world. Currently, there are about 4.5 billion people in Asia. By 2050, there will be about 5.3 billion. The two countries with the biggest populations are in Asia. They are China and India. China has about 1.35 billion people, and India has about 1.28 billion. Experts believe that by 2050, even though China will have a slightly smaller population—about 1.31 billion—India will have about 1.65 billion people.

What effects will this population growth have? Some are easy to guess. For example, we may not have enough food, oil, and gas. Also, we will probably have more air and water pollution. Other effects are more complicated. Studies show that when there are a lot of people in a small area, those people are not likely to talk to their neighbors. That's why people in small towns know their neighbors better than people in cities do. Will we all stop talking to each other in the future?

Some experts think that there will be 9 to 10 billion people on Earth by 2050. That means it will take only 12 to 14 years to add 1 billion more people to the population. It used to take much longer. It took 100 years for the population to grow from 1 to 2 billion. How many people will there be by the year 3000?

B. When we read large numbers with decimals like *1.2 billion*, we say *one point two billion*. Underline two examples of large numbers with decimals in the reading. Read them out loud.

Check Your Understanding

C. Answer the questions.

1. What is the fastest-growing area of the world?

   Africa
   _____

2. Which area of the world has the largest population today?

   _____

3. Which country has the largest population today?

   _____

4. How long did it take for the population to grow from 1 to 2 billion?

   _____

5. How long will it take to grow from about 7 billion to about 9 to 10 billion?

   _____

Vocabulary Strategy

Collocations with *take*

Collocations are sets of words that are used together. Learning collocations will help you increase your vocabulary quickly. You can use the verb *take* with many different words.

take time	take out the trash	take a class	take a nap
take notes	take a shower	take a test	take a picture
take place	take a break	take a look	

GO ONLINE for more practice

D. Complete each set of sentences with a phrase from the Vocabulary Strategy box.

1. I'm sleepy. I'm going to _____.

2. I didn't go to class today. Did you _____? Can I see them?

3. I want to learn how to cook. I'm going to _____ in the evenings.

4. I have to study tonight. I'm going to _____ in my chemistry class tomorrow.

5. Where's my cell phone? That tree is so pretty. I want to _____ of it.

Reading Strategy

Scan for Information

If you want to find specific information in a reading, you don't have to read the whole text carefully. You can scan the text to find the information. When you scan, you look over a text quickly and look for something specific, such as a number or a name.

GO ONLINE for more practice

E. Scan the text on page 100. Find the answer to each question.

1. How many people live in Asia? _____

2. How many people will there be in Asia in 2050? _____

3. How many people live in China? _____

4. How many people will there be in China in 2050? _____

5. How many people live in India? _____

6. How many people will there be in India in 2050? _____

Reading 2

A. Listen and read along.

What Do Global Cities Have in Common?

Stop and Think

What technology makes it easy for people in different countries to communicate?

These days, people all over the world **connect** with each other. Every day, technology allows people from different countries to communicate with each other. Things that happen in one part of the world **affect** other parts of the world. Large cities affect life all over the planet. These large cities are known as global cities. Some examples of global cities are London, New York, Hong Kong, Paris, Singapore, Tokyo, and Dubai. These places are different in many ways, but they also have a lot of the same characteristics.

Paris

Global cities are **centers** of **business**. A lot of **financial** companies and other large companies have offices in these cities. If you visit a global city, you can probably find an office for almost every important company in the world. People from small towns often work in the nearest global city because there are a lot of jobs. Global cities control the **economies** of the smaller cities and towns in their areas.

Dubai

Some of the world's best universities are in global cities. These universities often have more **international** students than other schools do. Some examples of these universities are the Sorbonne in Paris, King's College in London, the National University of Singapore, and the Hong Kong University of Science and Technology.

Global cities also have international populations. People from all over the world go to global cities for work and for school. If you walk down the street in a global city, you will probably hear several different languages. It's easy to travel to a global city because these cities have large international airports. These airports have a lot of flights to other global cities.

A lot of new ideas and important decisions take place in these cities. They have a lot of influence on the rest of the world. There are more global cities today than there were 20 years ago, and there will be more global cities in the future. Which cities do you think will become global cities in 10, 20, or 50 years?

London

Grammar in the Readings

Notice *more/less* + noun in the readings.

Use *more* with plural count nouns and noncount nouns to show that the amount of something has increased.

> *There will be **more global cities** in the future.*
> *We get **more information** online now.*

Use *less* with noncount nouns to show that the amount of something has decreased.

> *We get **less information** from books now.*

Notice *will* + verb in the readings.

Use *will* (*not*) before a verb to write about the future.

> *More people **will live** in cities in the future.*

Use *will* before *be* with adjectives and nouns.

> *The world population **will be** much bigger in 2050.*

GO ONLINE
for grammar
practice

Check Your Understanding

B. Complete the chart with information from the reading on pages 102–103. Write the three main characteristics about global cities. Then add details about each characteristic.

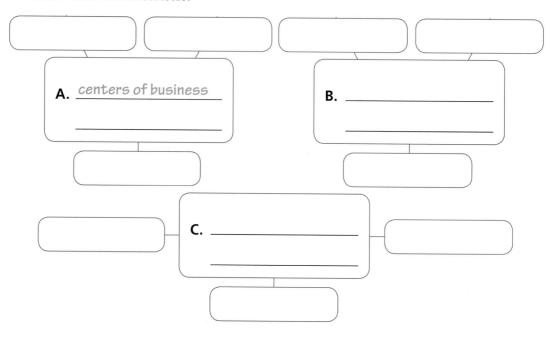

A. *centers of business*

B. _____

C. _____

Vocabulary Strategy: Collocations with *take*

C. Complete each sentence with a phrase from the box. You will not use all of the phrases.

take time	take out the trash	take a class	take a nap
take notes	take a shower	take a test	take a picture
take place	take a break	take a look	

1. This is an interesting chart. You should _____.

2. A lot of important decisions _____ in global cities.

3. The garbage can is full. Can you _____?

4. The population will not grow to 10 billion very quickly.

   It will _____.

5. I'm going to _____ for lunch. I will be back at work in about an hour.

Reading Strategy: Scan for Information

D. Scan the text on page 103. Find the answer to each question.

1. What are some examples of global cities?

_____

2. Where is the Sorbonne?

_____

3. Where is King's College?

_____

4. What is the name of a university in Hong Kong?

_____

⬤ **Make Connections:** Text to Text

A. Read each sentence. Does it describe Reading 1, Reading 2, or both? Write the letter of each sentence in the Venn diagram.

a. Some cities have a big influence on the world.

b. The population is growing much faster now than it was 100 years ago.

c. Developing countries are growing the fastest.

d. Some cities control the economies of their areas.

e. People from all over the world live in some cities.

f. As the world population grows, the population of global cities will also increase.

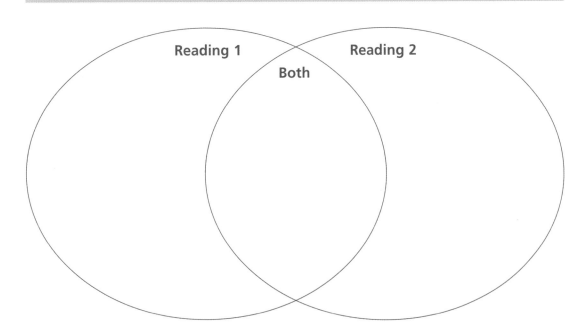

Reading 1   Reading 2
Both

B. Complete each sentence with information from the readings. Different answers are possible.

1. The fastest growing area of the world is _____.

2. The area with the biggest population is _____.

3. There are probably _____ global cities in Asia than there are in Africa.

Summarizing and Retelling

A. Complete the sentences with the words from the box. Some of the words have to be changed to fit the sentences. For example, *grow* has to be changed to *are growing*. Then read the sentences to a partner to summarize.

Nouns	Verbs	Adjectives	Adverbs
business center economy expert	affect connect grow	financial international	twice

1. Some parts of the world _____ faster than other parts of the world.

2. For example, some population growth _____ think that Africa will be _____ as big by 2050.

3. This fast growth will _____ the world in many different ways.

4. Technology allows people all over the world to _____ with each other easily. As a result, some big cities have become global cities.

5. Global cities have a few characteristics in common. One thing they have in common is they are important _____ of _____.

6. Also, there are a lot of _____ organizations in global cities, such as large banks.

7. Global cities control the _____ of smaller cities in their areas.

8. They also have _____ populations—people from all over the world live in global cities.

B. Answer the questions with a partner.

1. Do you think populations of global cities will grow quickly in the future? Why or why not?

2. Do you think there will be more global cities in Africa in the future? Why or why not?

Word Partners

business card

business person

business trip

good business

do business

big business

GO ONLINE
to practice
word partners

● Make Connections: Text to World

A. Answer the questions.

1. Why do you think some people want to live in global cities?

_____

_____

2. Why do you think some people don't want to live in global cities?

_____

_____

3. Some experts think that the population will not continue to grow forever. They think it will start to get smaller at some time in the future. What are some possible reasons that the population will start to get smaller?

_____

_____

B. Talk about your answers from Activity A with a partner and complete the chart with as many ideas as you can. Look at the Oxford 2000 keywords on page 133 and find five words to help you.

Reasons People Want to Live in Global Cities	Reasons People Do Not Want to Live in Global Cities

Chant

GO ONLINE for the Chapter 7 Vocabulary & Grammar Chant

CHAPTER 8

How Will We Work?

- /f/ and voiceless th /θ/ sounds
- Identify definitions
- Predict
- *could not; so that; can + verb*

▲ BEFORE READING ► Oxford 2000 🔑 words to talk about work

Learn Vocabulary

A. Match each description to the correct picture.

1. **Instead** means in the place of something.

   I usually have coffee in the morning, but today I think I'll have tea instead.

3. Your **environment** is the conditions in which you live, work, etc.

   I study at a library. It's a relaxing environment. It's very quiet and calm.

5. If something is **fun**, it is enjoyable.

   Children have fun playing at the park.

2. If something is **complicated**, it is difficult to understand because it has a lot of different parts or characteristics.

   This math problem is so complicated. I don't understand it at all.

4. If something is **physical**, it is a real thing that you can touch.

   Does your company have a physical office, or does everyone just communicate with each other online?

6. If you **require** something, you need it.

   My company requires visitors to get a visitor's pass.

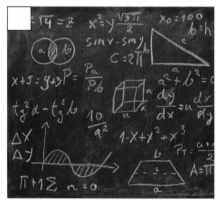

B. Read the descriptions and label the picture with the bold words.

1. If something is **full**, it has a lot of people or things in it. There is no more space.

   The parking lot is full of new cars.

2. A **factory** is a large building where things are made.

   I work in a car factory. We build cars.

3. A **machine** is a thing with moving parts that is made to do a job.

   Machines build some parts of the cars.

4. A **row** is a line of people or things.

   There are rows of new cars outside.

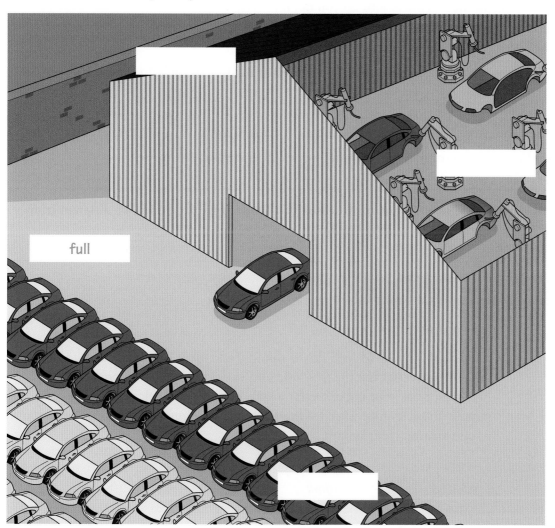

full

C. Complete each sentence with words from the box.

factory	fun	instead	machine	physical	requires	~~rows~~

1. There are ____rows____ of _____ in the _____. The machines make cars.

2. Everyone _____ some _____ exercise every day. It's good for your health.

3. I don't want to work. I want to do something _____ _____.

GO ONLINE
for more practice

Preview the Text

D. Look at the pictures on page 112. Write a short answer to each question.

1. What do you see in the pictures?

_____

2. Which of these types of work do you prefer?

_____

3. Which of these types of jobs do you not like? Why?

_____

E. Look at the text on page 112. Write a short answer to each question.

1. What is the title?

_____

2. What do you think is one way that work will change in the future?

_____

3. What do you think is one main reason that work in the future will be different from work today?

_____

Sounds of English

Spelling Connection

A. There are two ways to spell the /f/ sound: *f* and *ph*. It can be difficult to hear the difference between the /f/ sound and voiceless th /θ/. To pronounce the /f/ sound, place your upper teeth on your lower lip and release air from your mouth. To pronounce voiceless th /θ/, put your tongue between your teeth and release air from your mouth.

/f/ sound	voiceless th /θ/
physical	*think*
photo	*three*

B. Listen to the words. Circle the sound that you hear.

1. telephone	a. /f/	b. /θ/
2. thing	a. /f/	b. /θ/
3. fun	a. /f/	b. /θ/
4. third	a. /f/	b. /θ/
5. full	a. /f/	b. /θ/

● Make Connections: Text to Self

A. Answer the questions.

1. How do you use technology to communicate?

_____

2. Do you and the people you know go to specific places to work, or do you work from home?

_____

_____

3. Do you think you would like working from home? Why or why not?

_____

_____

_____

_____

B. What kinds of work do you think people can do from home? What kinds of work do you think people have to do at a specific place? Complete the chart with your ideas.

```
┌──────────────────┐      ┌──────────────────┐
│                  │      │                  │
└──────────────────┘      └──────────────────┘
           \                   /
          ┌──────────────────────┐
          │   Work from Home     │
          └──────────────────────┘
                     │
          ┌──────────────────────────┐
          │                          │
          └──────────────────────────┘

┌──────────────────┐      ┌──────────────────┐
│                  │      │                  │
└──────────────────┘      └──────────────────┘
           \                   /
          ┌──────────────────────┐
          │   Work at a          │
          │   Specific Place     │
          └──────────────────────┘
                     │
          ┌──────────────────────────┐
          │                          │
          └──────────────────────────┘
```

◉ Reading 1

A. Read the text on your own.

How Will We Work?

Stop and Think

What other places of work can you think of?

When you think of work, what do you imagine? Do you see **factory** workers putting food in boxes? Do you see supermarket employees or salespeople helping customers? Do you see business people working in cubicles? In the future, work will look much different. Work will be what you *do*, not where you *go*.

Experts believe that in the future, most people will have information jobs. In other words, most people will have jobs in technology. These people won't have to leave home in order to work. In the past, people couldn't communicate easily with employers and co-workers while they were at home. The only way that they could converse with people was by telephone. Today, we can communicate easily online. In the future, technology and the Internet will allow people to communicate even more easily with their employers and their co-workers.

people working in cubicles

When people have to commute—drive, ride a bike, walk, or take public transportation—to work, their offices will look very different from most offices today. Office buildings won't be **full** of **rows** of cubicles. Instead, there will be areas for casual, or informal, conversations, spaces for group work or meetings, and a few spaces for people to work alone. Experts also believe that these offices will be **fun environments**. Why? Companies will have to make their offices entertaining so that people will want to come into the office sometimes. Offices will have gyms for exercise, cafeterias with good food, and games for employees to play.

So what will happen to factory jobs, supermarket jobs, and other **physical** kinds of work? According to experts, robots and **machines** will do those kinds of jobs. You have probably already seen machines in supermarkets. They can do the jobs of supermarket cashiers. Many factories already use robots or robotic machines **instead** of human workers for many jobs.

a robot

people working in a factory

In the future, work will be much different. Will these changes make our lives easier? Will we work more or less than we do now? Will we be happier? No one really knows. We'll have to wait and see.

B. Underline each comma (,), period (.), question mark (?), dash (—), and exclamation point (!) in the reading.

C. Read the text with pauses to a partner. Use short pauses after commas. Use a long pause after periods, question marks, exclamation points, and dashes.

Check Your Understanding

D. Answer the questions.

1. What types of jobs will people have in the future?

_____

2. Where will most people work in the future?

_____

3. Why will people be able to work differently in the future?

_____

4. What are two ways that offices of the future will be different from offices of today?

_____

5. What kinds of jobs will be gone in the future? Why will these jobs be gone?

_____

_____

6. Some of the kinds of changes in the article are happening already. Where do you think these changes are happening, in small towns or big cities? Explain.

_____

_____

_____

Vocabulary Strategy

Identify Definitions
When you read a new word, you don't always have to look it up in a dictionary. You can sometimes find the definition near the new word. Finding the definition to a new word in the text will save you time and help you understand what you are reading. Sometimes a new word is separated from its definition by a comma (,) or a dash (—). Sometimes the definition comes in the sentence before or the sentence after.

GO ONLINE
for more
practice

E. Underline the definition of each bold word.

1. Experts believe that in the future, most people will have **information jobs**. In other words, most people will have <u>jobs in technology</u>.

2. When people do have to **commute**—drive, ride a bike, walk, or take public transportation—to work, their offices will look very different from most offices today.

3. Instead, there will be areas for **casual**, or informal, conversations, spaces for group work or meetings, and a few spaces for people to work alone.

4. Experts also believe that these offices will be fun environments. Why? Companies will have to make their offices **entertaining** so that people will want to come into the office sometimes.

5. The only way that they could **converse** with people was by telephone. Today, we can communicate easily online.

Reading Strategy

Predict

You can make predictions before you read and while you read. In other words, you can guess what the reading is going to tell you. Before you read, you can look at the pictures and read the title, headings, and first sentences of paragraphs to guess what the reading will say. While you read, you can stop after a sentence or a paragraph to predict what you will learn next. This will help you understand the reading better.

GO ONLINE
for more
practice

F. Look ahead to Reading 2 on page 115. Find the answer to each question.

1. What do you think this reading will be about?

_____

2. Read the first sentence of paragraph 2. What information do you think will come in this paragraph?

_____

3. Read the first sentence of paragraph 5. What kinds of tasks do you think new technology allows employers to track?

_____

◉ Reading 2

A. Listen and read along.

Tracking Work in the Future

In the past, almost everyone went to a physical place to work. According to some experts, in the future, most people will telecommute, or work from home, **instead**. Employers won't be able to see rows of employees working. So how will employers check that their employees are doing their jobs? With an app! There are several types of computer software for tracking work, or checking someone's work progress. Right now, a lot of people use these apps so that they can keep track of their own schedules. However, in the future, employers may use them more.

Stop and Think

How do you think employers will track people's work?

Some work-tracking apps are very easy. Users can say what they're doing and start a timer. When they're finished, they can stop the timer. At the end of the week, users can share the information from the tracker with their employers.

Other apps are more **complicated**. With these apps, you can schedule jobs. You can type in the name of a task and the time that you want to begin the task. The app will tell you when you have to begin each task. Then it will keep track of your time on the task. Some apps even create invoices, or bills, that users can send to employers so that they can get paid for their work.

Some apps allow employers to keep track of almost everything an employee does. With these apps, employers can read employees' emails and see what websites they visit. They can also see what employees type, how much time they spend away from their computers, and who works the fastest.

In the past, employers could see their employees working, but they could not keep track of every task. With new technology, they can. In the future, these apps will probably become more popular with employers and employees. Employers may **require** employees to use them so that they can track their work hours. The apps will show that employees are working, and it will also help employers understand how long different tasks take.

Grammar in the Readings

Notice *could not* in the reading.

Use *could not (couldn't)* to say that something was not able to happen in the past.

*In the past, people **couldn't** communicate easily with employers and co-workers while they were at home.*

Notice *so that* in the readings.

Writers use *so that* to show the purpose of an action. *So that* combines two subject-verb combinations.

> *A lot of people use trackers **so that** they can keep track of their own schedules.*

Notice *can* + verb in the readings.

Use *can* + verb to describe opportunities and skills that are true now.

> *Today, we **can communicate** easily online.*

GO ONLINE
for grammar
practice

Check Your Understanding

B. What can some tracking apps do? Complete the chart with information from the reading on page 115.

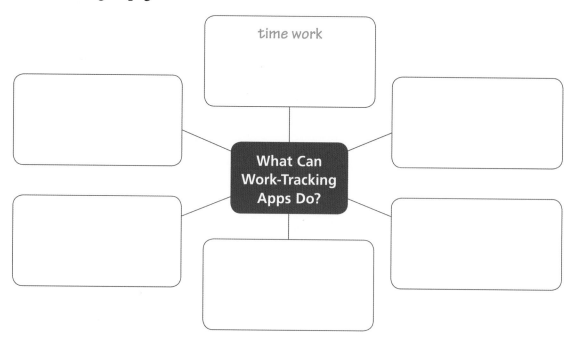

Recycle

the Vocabulary Strategy

Vocabulary Strategy: Identify Definitions

C. Underline the definition of each bold word.

1. With these apps, you can **schedule** tasks. You can <u>enter the name of a task and the time that you want to begin the task.</u>

2. Some apps even create **invoices**, or bills, that users can send to employers so that they can get paid for their work.

3. According to some experts, in the future, most people will **telecommute**, or work from home, instead.

4. With an **app**! There are several types of computer software for tracking work.

Reading Strategy: Predict

Recycle

the Reading
Strategy

D. Look at the reading on page 127 in Chapter 9. Find the answer to each question.

1. What do you think this reading will be about?

_____

2. Read the first sentence of paragraph 2. What information do you think will come in this paragraph?

_____

3. Read the first sentence of paragraph 6. What other changes will new technology bring?

_____

⬤ Make Connections: Text to Text

A. Read each sentence. Does it describe Reading 1, Reading 2, or both? Write the letter of each sentence in the Venn diagram.

a. Most people won't have to commute to work.

b. Employers will be able to track employees' tasks.

c. Employers and employees won't work in an office together.

d. Most offices won't have cubicles.

e. Offices will be fun and entertaining.

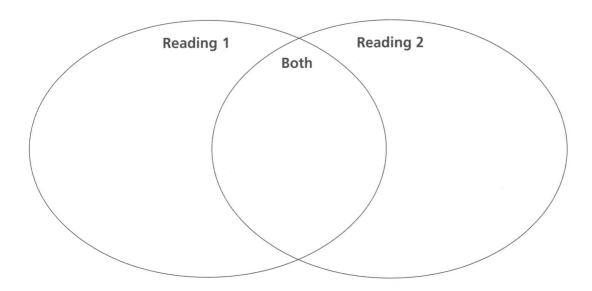

Reading 1   Both   Reading 2

B. Complete each sentence with information from the readings. Different answers are possible.

1. Most people in the future will have jobs related to _____.

2. _____ will make it possible for most people to work from home.

3. Employers will be able to use _____ to track employees' work.

Summarizing and Retelling

A. Complete the sentences with words from the box. Some of the words have to be changed to fit the sentences. For example, *environment* has to be changed to *environments*. Then read the sentences to a partner to retell the ideas.

Nouns	Verbs	Adjectives	Adverbs
factory environment machine row	require	complicated full fun physical	instead (of)

1. In the future, most people will work from home _____ of going to a _____ place for work.

2. People will have jobs related to technology. There will not be a lot of jobs in _____.

3. _____ will do certain jobs, like jobs that people do in factories.

4. Offices will look different in the future. They won't be _____ of _____ of cubicles.

5. Offices will be _____ and entertaining _____.

6. Employers won't be able to see their employees working. They may _____ their workers to use apps to keep track of their work.

7. Some of these apps are simple, but some are more _____.

B. Answer the questions with a partner.

1. You read about how work will change in the future. Do you think these changes will happen soon where you live? Why or why not?

2. Do you think employers should use apps to track employees' work? Why or why not?

Word Partners

physical place

physical contact

physical appearance

physical health

physical fitness

GO ONLINE
to practice
word partners

●● Make Connections: Text to World

A. Answer the questions.

1. Do you think that the changes from Reading 1 will make our lives easier or more difficult? Explain.

_____

_____

2. Do you think people will work more hours in the future or not? Explain.

_____

_____

3. Do you think work will be more enjoyable or less enjoyable in the future? Explain.

_____

_____

B. Look at the photo. Would you like to work in an office like this one? Explain why or why not.

Chant

GO ONLINE for the Chapter 8 Vocabulary & Grammar Chant

C. Talk about your answers to Activities A and B with a partner. Look at the Oxford 2000 keywords on page 133 and find five words to help you.

CHAPTER 9

What Will Our World Look Like?

- Consonant clusters
- Word families
- Comparison signal words
- *can*, *may*, and *will*

▲ BEFORE READING ▶ Oxford 2000 🔑 words to talk about innovation

Learn Vocabulary

A. Match each description to the correct picture.

1. **Nearby** means close, not far away in distance.

   I like my neighborhood. There's a great park nearby.

3. **Material** is something that can be used for making or doing something.

   I use different materials in my art. I use paint, paper, wood, and other things.

5. If you **create** something, you cause something new to happen or exist.

   I created a new pizza recipe. I used a lot of different things from my refrigerator.

2. If something is **empty**, it has nothing or nobody inside it.

   The room is empty. No one is in there.

4. If something happens **suddenly**, it happens quickly and unexpectedly.

   I had to stop quickly because a little boy suddenly ran in front of my car.

6. If a mistake or accident is your **fault**, you made it happen.

   The accident was my fault. I wasn't paying attention to where I was going.

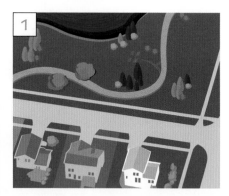

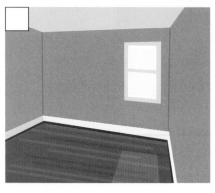

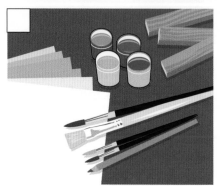

B. Match each description to the correct picture.

1. If something is **artificial**, it is not natural but made by people.

    A lot of junk food, such as cookies and candy, has artificial colors in it. The colors aren't natural.

2. If something is **harmful**, it causes injury or damage.

    Some old cars are harmful to the environment because they use a lot of gas and make a lot of pollution.

3. A **process** is a number of actions for doing or making something.

    The process is complicated. There are a lot of steps.

4. If something is **helpful**, it makes something easier or better.

    Recycling is helpful to the environment.

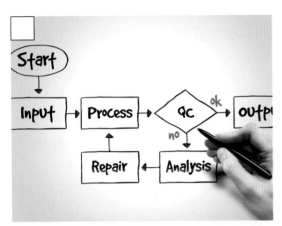

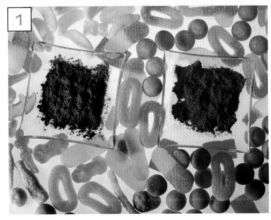

Oxford 2000 🔑

Use the Oxford 2000 list on page 133 to find more words to describe the pictures on these pages. Share your words with a partner.

C. Read each pair of words. Do they have similar or different meanings?

1. artificial, real	similar	(different)
2. helpful, useful	similar	different
3. create, make	similar	different
4. harmful, good	similar	different
5. nearby, far	similar	different
6. suddenly, quickly	similar	different
7. empty, full	similar	different

GO ONLINE for more practice

Preview the Text

D. Look at the pictures on page 124. Write a short answer to each question.

1. What do you see in the pictures?

_____

2. Why do you think these pictures are included with the article?

_____

E. Look at the text on page 124. Write a short answer to each question.

1. What is the title?

_____

2. What do you think buildings of the future will look like? Why?

_____

3. Where do you think the biggest changes will happen—in cities or in small towns? Why?

_____

Sounds of English

Spelling Connection

A. Consonant clusters are groups of two or more consonants. They can be difficult to hear and to pronounce. There is no added sound between the consonants.

create	*nearby*
harmful	*suddenly*

B. Listen to the words. Circle the sound that you hear.

1. (mpt)   ft
2. lapf   lpf
3. lpt   lt
4. mpl   ml
5. tst   nst

⬤ Make Connections: Text to Self

A. Answer the questions.

1. What are tall buildings in your city made of?

_____

2. Why do you think builders used these materials?

_____

_____

3. Researchers are trying to find and create other materials for building. Why do you think they are doing this?

_____

_____

_____

_____

B. What kinds of materials do people use to build tall buildings? Complete the chart with your ideas.

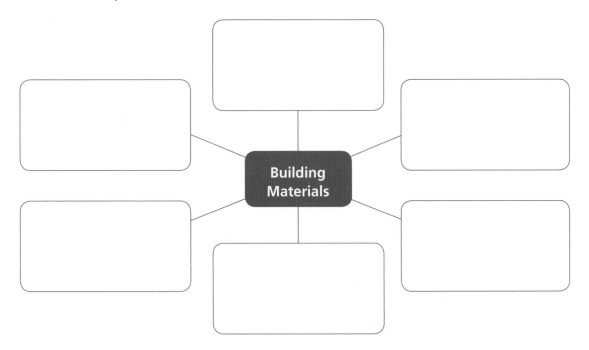

▲▲ DURING READING
▶ Vocabulary strategy: Word families
▶ Reading strategy: Comparison signal words

◉ Reading 1

A. Read the text on your own.

What Will Our World Be Made Of?

Stop and Think

Why do you think most people live in big cities?

concrete

steel

glue

Today, more than half of the world's population lives in big cities. Some experts believe that by 2050, 66 percent of the global population will live in cities. There will be a lot of people in small areas, so they will have to live in tall buildings. What will these tall buildings of the future be made of?

wood

Like today's tall buildings, buildings of the future may be made mostly of concrete and steel. However, the **processes** of making concrete and steel are bad for the environment. Therefore, scientists all over the world are working to **create** new building **materials**. They want these building materials to be strong and good for the environment.

Researchers at the Massachusetts Institute of Technology in Cambridge, Massachusetts, are creating **artificial** bone. Why? Bone is very strong. Similar to real bone, this new material is also strong. Unlike bone, it can last a long time. It is also better for the environment than steel and concrete.

Researchers in different areas of the world are using bacteria to create new building materials. Bacteria are very small living things. They are everywhere, and some are **harmful** while some are **helpful**. These researchers believe that this material will be very strong and will also be able to grow. It will be natural, so just like artificial bone, it will not be harmful to the environment.

Similar to these researchers, a Canadian architect named Michael Green also wants to stop using concrete and steel to build tall buildings. However, he doesn't want to create a new material. He wants to use an old one—wood. He and his team have developed a process for making large pieces of very strong wood for building. They use a special glue to put several small pieces of wood together. According to Green, using wood is good for the environment because wood is natural. You just have to use fast-growing trees. That way, you don't have to cut down old trees and destroy forests.

No one really knows what buildings of the future will be made of. However, building materials of the future will probably be good for the Earth.

B. Underline the main ideas of paragraphs 2 through 5.

C. Read the text again. Pause after every few sentences to make sure that you understood what you just read. Then read the text quickly all the way through to check your answers from Activity B.

Check Your Understanding

D. Answer the questions.

1. Why are some scientists trying to create new building materials?

   Concrete and steel are bad for the environment.

2. What are two new building materials described in the reading? Why might they be better than concrete and steel?

3. What kind of material does Michael Green want to use for tall buildings in the future? Why does Michael Green want to use this material?

4. How did Michael Green and his team make this material new and different?

GO ONLINE
for more
practice

Vocabulary Strategy

Word Families

Word families are groups of words that have the same base word. The words in word families are usually different parts of speech. Learning word families instead of single words can help you learn a large amount of vocabulary quickly. Look at the examples.

> noun: *population*
> adjective: *populated*
> verb: *populate*

E. Complete the chart. Use a dictionary for help.

Nouns	Verbs	Adjectives	Adverbs
process	process	processed	
_____		environmental	environmentally
scientist		_____	scientifically
_____	strengthen	_____	strongly
creation	_____	_____	_____
harm	_____	_____	harmfully
development	_____	developed	

GO ONLINE
for more
practice

Reading Strategy

Comparison Signal Words
Writers use certain words and phrases to compare two things or talk about how they are alike. Learning how something is like another thing can help you understand it better. Here are some examples of words that signal comparison.

similar to   *similarly*   *like*   *alike*   *just like*

F. Look at the text on page 124. Find and underline an example of each word or phrase. Then write the two compared things.

1. like

_____

2. similar to (paragraph 3)

_____

3. just like

_____

4. similar to (paragraph 5)

_____

◉ Reading 2

A. Listen and read along.

Will We Still Drive?

In some movies about the future, cars can drive themselves. They don't need drivers. Will we see self-driving cars in the future? Maybe. Right now, a few different companies are working on creating self-driving cars…and they have had some success.

The car company Audi recently sent a self-driving car on a 560-mile trip on freeways. The car safely took passengers from Silicon Valley in California to Las Vegas, Nevada. The car uses technology to "see" the road, choose a path, and change lanes. It knows where other cars are and how close they are. With all this technology, though, the car needed a driver for a small part of the time. Passengers had to become drivers near big cities with a lot of traffic and fast lane changes.

A car by BMW can park itself. Some of today's cars already have self-parking technology, but this car can drive through a parking garage, find a parking space, and park in it. Similar to the first car, this car can tell how close other cars are. It also knows when people are walking **nearby**.

Google's self-driving cars have already driven over a million miles on city streets. This car can drive up to 25 miles per hour. Like the other two cars, this car knows when people or other cars are nearby. This company hopes to make its cars available to the public soon.

Even if these cars become available, we won't **suddenly** see them everywhere. The laws for these cars will be very complicated. For example, if a self-driving car is **empty** and it hits someone, whose **fault** is it?

We may or may not have self-driving cars soon, but we will see some other exciting changes in the future. For example, some cars of the future will have solar panels. These panels will get energy from the sun so they can run without gas or any other type of fuel. Other cars will run on air. Just like solar-powered cars, these cars will be good for the environment.

> **Stop and Think**
>
> What else do you think cars of the future will be able to do?

Grammar in the Readings

Notice *can*, *may*, and *will* in the readings.

Use *can* + verb to say that something is possible in the present.

*Right now, some cars **can help** drivers park.*

Use *may* + verb to say that something is possible in the future.

*In the future, cars **may drive** themselves.*

Use *will* + verb to say that something is certain in the future.

*We **will see** a lot of exciting changes in cars in the future.*

GO ONLINE
for grammar
practice

Check Your Understanding

B. What can some cars of the future do? Complete the chart with information from the reading on page 127.

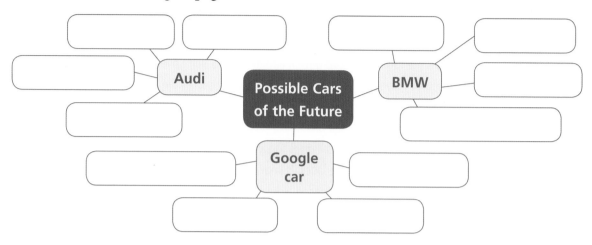

C. Answer the questions.

1. Will we see a lot of self-driving cars on the road soon? Why or why not?

_____

2. What is one thing that the Audi *cannot* do but the BMW *can* do?

_____

3. What is one thing that the Google car *cannot* do but the Audi *can* do?

_____

4. What is one thing that all three cars *can* do?

_____

5. Besides driving themselves, what other things will cars of the future do?

_____

Vocabulary Strategy: Word Families

Recycle

the Vocabulary Strategy

D. Complete the chart. Use a dictionary for help.

Nouns	Verbs	Adjectives	Adverbs
	drive	driven	
_____	change	changed, changing	
	know	known, knowing	knowingly
		_____	suddenly
_____	_____	empty	emptily

Reading Strategy: Comparison Signal Words

Recycle

the Reading
Strategy

E. Look at the text on page 127. Find and underline an example of each word or phrase. Write the two compared things.

1. similar to _____

2. like _____

3. just like _____

◖ Make Connections: Text to Text

A. Read each sentence. Does it describe Reading 1, Reading 2, or both? Write the letter of each sentence in the Venn diagram.

a. Scientists are developing new building materials.

b. One architect wants to use wood for building instead of concrete and steel.

c. The world around us may look very different in the future.

d. In the future, people will try to make things that are good for the environment.

e. In the future, cars may be able to park and drive themselves.

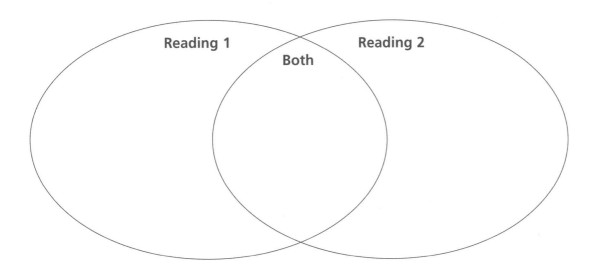

B. Complete each sentence with information from the readings. Different answers are possible.

1. Scientists and architects are researching new building _____.

   They will be good for _____.

2. In the future, you might not ever have to learn how to _____ a car.

3. You might ride in a _____ to a building made of

   _____ in the future.

Summarizing and Retelling

A. Complete the sentences with the words from the box. Some of the words have to be changed to fit the sentences. For example, *material* has to be changed to *materials*. Then read the sentences to a partner to summarize.

Nouns	Verbs	Adjectives	Adverbs
fault material process	create	artificial empty harmful helpful nearby	suddenly

1. Scientists are trying to _____ new building _____.

2. One of these things is _____ bone. It is like real bone, but it is made by scientists.

3. These materials are good for the environment. They are _____. They are not _____.

4. These new materials will be better for the environment than concrete and steel are. The _____ for making concrete and steel are bad for the environment.

5. Several companies are developing self-driving cars. Some of these cars can park themselves with no drivers. The cars are _____ when they park.

6. These self-parking and self-driving cars know when a person or another car is _____.

7. Experts believe these cars will slowly become popular. They don't think that we are _____ going to see self-driving cars everywhere.

8. One reason for this is that the laws will be complicated. For example, if two empty self-driving cars have an accident, it will be difficult to say whose _____ it is.

B. Answer the questions with a partner.

1. Which building material do you think will be most popular in 100 years—concrete and steel, wood, bacteria, artificial bone, or something else? Why?

2. When do you think most people will have self-driving cars? Why?

Word Partners

building material

man-made material

reading material

writing material

instructional material

useful material

GO ONLINE
to practice
word partners

⬤ Make Connections: Text to World

A. Answer the questions.

1. Which of the building materials from Reading 1 do you think is the best? Explain.

_____

_____

2. Do you think self-driving cars will be safer or more dangerous than regular cars? Explain.

_____

_____

3. Do you think work will be easier or more difficult in the future? Explain.

_____

_____

B. Talk about your answers from Activity A with a partner and complete the chart with as many ideas as you can. Look at the Oxford 2000 keywords on page 133 and find five words to help you.

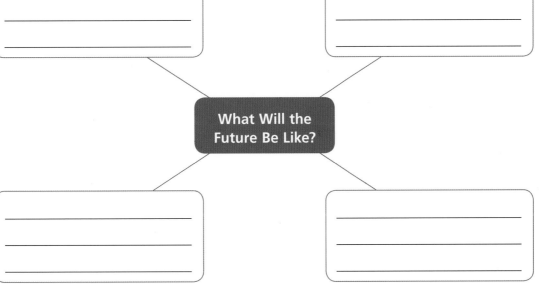

What Will the Future Be Like?

Chant

GO ONLINE for the Chapter 9 Vocabulary & Grammar Chant

Look at the word bank for Unit 3. Check (✓) the words you know. Circle the words you want to learn better.

OXFORD 2000 🔑

Adjectives	Nouns	Verbs
artificial	business	affect
complicated	center	connect
empty	economy	create
financial	environment	grow
full	expert	require
fun	factory	
harmful	fault	
helpful	machine	
international	material	
nearby	process	
physical	row	

PRACTICE WITH THE OXFORD 2000 🔑

A. Use the words in the chart. Match adjectives with nouns.

1. _complicated process_   2. _____

3. _____   4. _____

5. _____

B. Use the words in the chart. Match verbs with nouns.

1. _connect experts_   2. _____

3. _____   4. _____

5. _____

C. Use the words in the chart. Match verbs with adjective noun partners.

1. _require physical materials_   2. _____

3. _____   4. _____

5. _____

This is a list of the 2000 most important and useful words to learn at this stage in your language learning. These words have been carefully chosen by a group of language experts and experienced teachers, who have judged the words to be important and useful for three reasons.

- Words that are used very **frequently** (= very often) in English are included in this list. Frequency information has been gathered from the American English section of the Oxford English Corpus, which is a collection of written and spoken texts containing over 2 billion words.

- The keywords are frequent across a **range** of different types of text. This means that the keywords are often used in a variety of contexts, not just in newspapers or in scientific articles, for example.

- The list includes some important words which are very **familiar** to most users of English, even though they are not used very frequently. These include, for example, words which are useful for explaining what you mean when you do not know the exact word for something.

Names of people, places, etc. beginning with a capital letter are not included in the list of 2000 keywords. Keywords which are not included in the list are numbers, days of the week, and the months of the year.

A

a, an *indefinite article*
ability *n.*
able *adj.*
about *adv., prep.*
above *prep., adv.*
absolutely *adv.*
academic *adj.*
accept *v.*
acceptable *adj.*
accident *n.*
   by accident
according to *prep.*
account *n.*
accurate *adj.*
accuse *v.*
achieve *v.*
achievement *n.*
acid *n.*
across *adv., prep.*
act *n., v.*
action *n.*
active *adj.*
activity *n.*
actor, actress *n.*
actual *adj.*
actually *adv.*
add *v.*
address *n.*
admire *v.*
admit *v.*
adult *n.*
advanced *adj.*
advantage *n.*
adventure *n.*
advertisement *n.*
advice *n.*

advise *v.*
affect *v.*
afford *v.*
afraid *adj.*
after *prep., conj., adv.*
afternoon *n.*
afterward *adv.*
again *adv.*
against *prep.*
age *n.*
   aged *adj.*
ago *adv.*
agree *v.*
agreement *n.*
ahead *adv.*
aim *n., v.*
air *n.*
airplane *n.*
airport *n.*
alarm *n.*
alcohol *n.*
alcoholic *adj.*
alive *adj.*
all *adj., pron., adv.*
allow *v.*
all right *adj., adv.,*
   exclamation
almost *adv.*
alone *adj., adv.*
along *prep., adv.*
alphabet *n.*
already *adv.*
also *adv.*
although *conj.*
always *adv.*
among *prep.*
amount *n.*

amuse *v.*
analyze *v.*
analysis *n.*
ancient *adj.*
and *conj.*
anger *n.*
angle *n.*
angry *adj.*
animal *n.*
announce *v.*
another *adj., pron.*
answer *n., v.*
any *adj., pron., adv.*
anymore *(also* any more*)*
   adv.
anyone *(also* anybody*)*
   pron.
anything *pron.*
anyway *adv.*
anywhere *adv.*
apart *adv.*
apartment *n.*
apparently *adv.*
appear *v.*
appearance *n.*
apple *n.*
apply *v.*
appointment *n.*
appreciate *v.*
appropriate *adj.*
approve *v.*
area *n.*
argue *v.*
argument *n.*
arm *n.*
army *n.*
around *adv., prep.*

arrange *v.*
arrangement *n.*
arrest *v.*
arrive *v.*
arrow *n.*
art *n.*
article *n.*
artificial *adj.*
artist *n.*
artistic *adj.*
as *prep., conj.*
ashamed *adj.*
ask *v.*
asleep *adj.*
at *prep.*
atmosphere *n.*
atom *n.*
attach *v.*
attack *n., v.*
attention *n.*
attitude *n.*
attract *v.*
attractive *adj.*
aunt *n.*
authority *n.*
available *adj.*
average *adj., n.*
avoid *v.*
awake *adj.*
aware *adj.*
away *adv.*

B

baby *n.*
back *n., adj., adv.*
backward *adv.*
bad *adj.*

badly *adv.*
bag *n.*
bake *v.*
balance *n.*
ball *n.*
band *n.*
bank *n.*
bar *n.*
base *n., v.*
baseball *n.*
basic *adj.*
basis *n.*
bath *n.*
bathroom *n.*
be *v.*
beach *n.*
bear *v.*
beard *n.*
beat *v.*
beautiful *adj.*
beauty *n.*
because *conj.*
become *v.*
bed *n.*
bedroom *n.*
beer *n.*
before *prep., conj., adv.*
begin *v.*
beginning *n.*
behave *v.*
behavior *n.*
behind *prep., adv.*
belief *n.*
believe *v.*
bell *n.*
belong *v.*
below *prep., adv.*
belt *n.*
bend *v.*
benefit *n.*
beside *prep.*
best *adj., adv., n.*
better *adj., adv.*
between *prep., adv.*
beyond *prep., adv.*
bicycle *n.*
big *adj.*
bill *n.*
bird *n.*
birth *n.*
birthday *n.*
bite *v.*
bitter *adj.*
black *adj.*
blame *v.*
block *n.*
blood *n.*
blow *v., n.*
blue *adj., n.*

board *n.*
boat *n.*
body *n.*
boil *v.*
bomb *n., v.*
bone *n.*
book *n.*
boot *n.*
border *n.*
bored *adj.*
boring *adj.*
born: be born *v.*
borrow *v.*
boss *n.*
both *adj., pron.*
bother *v.*
bottle *n.*
bottom *n.*
bowl *n.*
box *n.*
boy *n.*
boyfriend *n.*
brain *n.*
branch *n.*
brave *adj.*
bread *n.*
break *v.*
breakfast *n.*
breath *n.*
breathe *v.*
brick *n.*
bridge *n.*
brief *adj.*
bright *adj.*
bring *v.*
broken *adj.*
brother *n.*
brown *adj., n.*
brush *n., v.*
bubble *n.*
build *v.*
building *n.*
bullet *n.*
burn *v.*
burst *v.*
bury *v.*
bus *n.*
bush *n.*
business *n.*
busy *adj.*
but *conj.*
butter *n.*
button *n.*
buy *v.*
by *prep.*
bye *exclamation*

C

cabinet *n.*

cake *n.*
calculate *v.*
call *v., n.*
calm *adj.*
camera *n.*
camp *n., v.*
can *modal v., n.*
cancel *v.*
candy *n.*
capable *adj.*
capital *n.*
car *n.*
card *n.*
care *n., v.*
   take care of
   care for
career *n.*
careful *adj.*
carefully *adv.*
careless *adj.*
carelessly *adv.*
carry *v.*
case *n.*
   in case (of)
cash *n.*
cat *n.*
catch *v.*
cause *n., v.*
CD *n.*
ceiling *n.*
celebrate *v.*
cell *n.*
cell phone *n.*
cent *n.*
center *n.*
centimeter *n.*
central *adj.*
century *n.*
ceremony *n.*
certain *adj.*
certainly *adv.*
chain *n., v.*
chair *n.*
challenge *n.*
chance *n.*
change *v., n.*
character *n.*
characteristic *n.*
charge *n., v.*
charity *n.*
chase *v., n.*
cheap *adj.*
cheat *v.*
check *v., n.*
cheek *n.*
cheese *n.*
chemical *adj., n.*
chemistry *n.*
chest *n.*

chicken *n.*
chief *adj., n.*
child *n.*
childhood *n.*
chin *n.*
chocolate *n.*
choice *n.*
choose *v.*
church *n.*
cigarette *n.*
circle *n.*
citizen *n.*
city *n.*
class *n.*
clean *adj., v.*
clear *adj., v.*
clearly *adv.*
climate *n.*
climb *v.*
clock *n.*
close /kloʊs/ *adj., adv.*
close /kloʊz/ *v.*
closed *adj.*
cloth *n.*
clothes *n.*
clothing *n.*
cloud *n.*
club *n.*
coast *n.*
coat *n.*
coffee *n.*
coin *n.*
cold *adj., n.*
collect *v.*
collection *n.*
college *n.*
color *n., v.*
column *n.*
combination *n.*
combine *v.*
come *v.*
comfortable *adj.*
command *n.*
comment *n., v.*
common *adj.*
communicate *v.*
communication *n.*
community *n.*
company *n.*
compare *v.*
comparison *n.*
competition *n.*
complain *v.*
complaint *n.*
complete *adj.*
completely *adv.*
complicated *adj.*
computer *n.*
concentrate *v.*

concert *n.*
conclusion *n.*
condition *n.*
confidence *n.*
confident *adj.*
confuse *v.*
confused *adj.*
connect *v.*
connection *n.*
conscious *adj.*
consider *v.*
consist *v.*
constant *adj.*
contact *n., v.*
contain *v.*
container *n.*
continent *n.*
continue *v.*
continuous *adj.*
contract *n.*
contrast *n.*
contribute *v.*
control *n., v.*
convenient *adj.*
conversation *n.*
convince *v.*
cook *v.*
cookie *n.*
cooking *n.*
cool *adj.*
copy *n., v.*
corner *n.*
correct *adj., v.*
correctly *adv.*
cost *n., v.*
cotton *n.*
cough *v.*
could *modal v.*
count *v.*
country *n.*
county *n.*
couple *n.*
course *n.*
   of course
court *n.*
cousin *n.*
cover *v., n.*
covering *n.*
cow *n.*
crack *v.*
crash *n., v.*
crazy *adj.*
cream *n., adj.*
create *v.*
credit card *n.*
crime *n.*
criminal *adj., n.*
crisis *n.*
criticism *n.*

criticize *v.*
cross *v.*
crowd *n.*
cruel *adj.*
crush *v.*
cry *v.*
culture *n.*
cup *n.*
curly *adj.*
curve *n.*
curved *adj.*
custom *n.*
customer *n.*
cut *v., n.*

D
dad *n.*
damage *n., v.*
dance *n., v.*
dancer *n.*
danger *n.*
dangerous *adj.*
dark *adj., n.*
date *n.*
daughter *n.*
day *n.*
dead *adj.*
deal *v.*
dear *adj.*
death *n.*
debt *n.*
decide *v.*
decision *n.*
decorate *v.*
deep *adj.*
deeply *adv.*
defeat *v.*
definite *adj.*
definitely *adv.*
definition *n.*
degree *n.*
deliberately *adv.*
deliver *v.*
demand *n., v.*
dentist *n.*
deny *v.*
department *n.*
depend *v.*
depression *n.*
describe *v.*
description *n.*
desert *n.*
deserve *v.*
design *n., v.*
desk *n.*
despite *prep.*
destroy *v.*
detail *n.*
   in detail

determination *n.*
determined *adj.*
develop *v.*
development *n.*
device *n.*
diagram *n.*
dictionary *n.*
die *v.*
difference *n.*
different *adj.*
difficult *adj.*
difficulty *n.*
dig *v.*
dinner *n.*
direct *adj., adv., v.*
direction *n.*
directly *adv.*
dirt *n.*
dirty *adj.*
disadvantage *n.*
disagree *v.*
disagreement *n.*
disappear *v.*
disappoint *v.*
disaster *n.*
discover *v.*
discuss *v.*
discussion *n.*
disease *n.*
disgusting *adj.*
dish *n.*
dishonest *adj.*
disk *n.*
distance *n.*
distant *adj.*
disturb *v.*
divide *v.*
division *n.*
divorce *n., v.*
do *v., auxiliary v.*
doctor *n. (abbr.* Dr.)
document *n.*
dog *n.*
dollar *n.*
door *n.*
dot *n.*
double *adj.*
doubt *n.*
down *adv., prep.*
downstairs *adv., adj.*
downward *adv.*
draw *v.*
drawer *n.*
drawing *n.*
dream *n., v.*
dress *n., v.*
drink *n., v.*
drive *v., n.*
driver *n.*

drop *v., n.*
drug *n.*
dry *adj., v.*
during *prep.*
dust *n.*
duty *n.*
DVD *n.*

E
each *adj., pron.*
each other *pron.*
ear *n.*
early *adj., adv.*
earn *v.*
earth *n.*
easily *adv.*
east *n., adj., adv.*
eastern *adj.*
easy *adj.*
eat *v.*
economic *adj.*
economy *n.*
edge *n.*
educate *v.*
education *n.*
effect *n.*
effort *n.*
e.g. *abbr.*
egg *n.*
either *adj., pron., adv.*
election *n.*
electric *adj.*
electrical *adj.*
electricity *n.*
electronic *adj.*
else *adv.*
e-mail *(also* email*) n., v.*
embarrass *v.*
embarrassed *adj.*
emergency *n.*
emotion *n.*
employ *v.*
employment *n.*
empty *adj.*
encourage *v.*
end *n., v.*
   in the end
enemy *n.*
energy *n.*
engine *n.*
enjoy *v.*
enjoyable *adj.*
enjoyment *n.*
enough *adj., pron., adv.*
enter *v.*
entertain *v.*
entertainment *n.*
enthusiasm *n.*
enthusiastic *adj.*

The Oxford 2000 List of Keywords

entrance *n.*
environment *n.*
equal *adj.*
equipment *n.*
error *n.*
escape *v.*
especially *adv.*
essential *adj.*
etc. *abbr.*
even *adv.*
evening *n.*
event *n.*
ever *adv.*
every *adj.*
everybody *pron.*
everyone *pron.*
everything *pron.*
everywhere *adv.*
evidence *n.*
evil *adj.*
exact *adj.*
exactly *adv.*
exaggerate *v.*
exam *n.*
examination *n.*
examine *v.*
example *n.*
excellent *adj.*
except *prep.*
exchange *v., n.*
excited *adj.*
excitement *n.*
exciting *adj.*
excuse *n., v.*
exercise *n.*
exist *v.*
exit *n.*
expect *v.*
expensive *adj.*
experience *n., v.*
experiment *n.*
expert *n.*
explain *v.*
explanation *n.*
explode *v.*
explore *v.*
explosion *n.*
expression *n.*
extra *adj., adv.*
extreme *adj.*
extremely *adv.*
eye *n.*

F

face *n., v.*
fact *n.*
factory *n.*
fail *v.*
failure *n.*

fair *adj.*
fall *v., n.*
false *adj.*
familiar *adj.*
family *n.*
famous *adj.*
far *adv., adj.*
farm *n.*
farmer *n.*
fashion *n.*
fashionable *adj.*
fast *adj., adv.*
fasten *v.*
fat *adj., n.*
father *n.*
fault *n.*
favor *n.*
    in favor
favorite *adj., n.*
fear *n., v.*
feather *n.*
feature *n.*
feed *v.*
feel *v.*
feeling *n.*
female *adj.*
fence *n.*
festival *n.*
few *adj., pron.*
    a few
field *n.*
fight *v., n.*
figure *n.*
file *n.*
fill *v.*
film *n.*
final *adj.*
finally *adv.*
financial *adj.*
find *v.*
    find out sth
fine *adj.*
finger *n.*
finish *v.*
fire *n., v.*
firm *n., adj.*
firmly *adv.*
first *adj., adv., n.*
    at first
fish *n.*
fit *v., adj.*
fix *v.*
fixed *adj.*
flag *n.*
flame *n.*
flash *v.*
flat *adj.*
flavor *n.*
flight *n.*

float *v.*
flood *n.*
floor *n.*
flour *n.*
flow *v.*
flower *n.*
fly *v.*
fold *v.*
follow *v.*
food *n.*
foot *n.*
football *n.*
for *prep.*
force *n., v.*
foreign *adj.*
forest *n.*
forever *adv.*
forget *v.*
forgive *v.*
fork *n.*
form *n., v.*
formal *adj.*
forward *adv.*
frame *n.*
free *adj., v., adv.*
freedom *n.*
freeze *v.*
fresh *adj.*
friend *n.*
friendly *adj.*
friendship *n.*
frighten *v.*
from *prep.*
front *n., adj.*
    in front
frozen *adj.*
fruit *n.*
fry *v.*
fuel *n.*
full *adj.*
fully *adv.*
fun *n., adj.*
funny *adj.*
fur *n.*
furniture *n.*
further *adj., adv.*
future *n., adj.*

G

gain *v.*
gallon *n.*
game *n.*
garbage *n.*
garden *n.*
gas *n.*
gate *n.*
general *adj.*
    in general
generally *adv.*

generous *adj.*
gentle *adj.*
gently *adv.*
gentleman *n.*
get *v.*
gift *n.*
girl *n.*
girlfriend *n.*
give *v.*
glass *n.*
glasses *n.*
global *adj.*
glove *n.*
go *v.*
goal *n.*
god *n.*
gold *n., adj.*
good *adj., n.*
goodbye *exclamation*
goods *n.*
govern *v.*
government *n.*
grade *n., v.*
grain *n.*
gram *n.*
grammar *n.*
grandchild *n.*
grandfather *n.*
grandmother *n.*
grandparent *n.*
grass *n.*
grateful *adj.*
gray *adj., n.*
great *adj.*
green *adj., n.*
groceries *n.*
ground *n.*
group *n.*
grow *v.*
growth *n.*
guard *n., v.*
guess *v.*
guest *n.*
guide *n.*
guilty *adj.*
gun *n.*

H

habit *n.*
hair *n.*
half *n., adj., pron., adv.*
hall *n.*
hammer *n.*
hand *n.*
handle *v., n.*
hang *v.*
happen *v.*
happiness *n.*
happy *adj.*

hard *adj., adv.*
hardly *adv.*
harm *n., v.*
harmful *adj.*
hat *n.*
hate *v., n.*
have *v.*
    have to *modal v.*
he *pron.*
head *n.*
health *n.*
healthy *adj.*
hear *v.*
heart *n.*
heat *n., v.*
heavy *adj.*
height *n.*
hello *exclamation*
help *v., n.*
helpful *adj.*
her *pron., adj.*
here *adv.*
hers *pron.*
herself *pron.*
hide *v.*
high *adj., adv.*
highly *adv.*
high school *n.*
highway *n.*
hill *n.*
him *pron.*
himself *pron.*
hire *v.*
his *adj., pron.*
history *n.*
hit *v., n.*
hold *v., n.*
hole *n.*
holiday *n.*
home *n., adv..*
honest *adj.*
hook *n.*
hope *v., n.*
horn *n.*
horse *n.*
hospital *n.*
hot *adj.*
hotel *n.*
hour *n.*
house *n.*
how *adv.*
however *adv.*
huge *adj.*
human *adj., n.*
humor *n.*
hungry *adj.*
hunt *v.*
hurry *v., n.*
hurt *v.*

husband *n.*

I

I *pron.*
ice *n.*
idea *n.*
identify *v.*
if *conj.*
ignore *v.*
illegal *adj.*
illegally *adv.*
illness *n.*
image *n.*
imagination *n.*
imagine *v.*
immediate *adj.*
immediately *adv.*
impatient *adj.*
importance *n.*
important *adj.*
impossible *adj.*
impress *v.*
impression *n.*
improve *v.*
improvement *n.*
in *prep., adv.*
inch *n.*
include *v.*
including *prep.*
increase *v., n.*
indeed *adv.*
independent *adj.*
individual *adj.*
industry *n.*
infection *n.*
influence *n.*
inform *v.*
informal *adj.*
information *n.*
injure *v.*
injury *n.*
insect *n.*
inside *prep., adv., n., adj.*
instead *adv., prep.*
instruction *n.*
instrument *n.*
insult *v., n.*
intelligent *adj.*
intend *v.*
intention *n.*
interest *n., v.*
interested *adj.*
interesting *adj.*
international *adj.*
Internet *n.*
interrupt *v.*
interview *n.*
into *prep.*
introduce *v.*

introduction *n.*
invent *v.*
investigate *v.*
invitation *n.*
invite *v.*
involve *v.*
iron *n.*
island *n.*
issue *n.*
it *pron.*
item *n.*
its *adj.*
itself *pron.*

J

jacket *n.*
jeans *n.*
jewelry *n.*
job *n.*
join *v.*
joke *n., v.*
judge *n., v.*
judgment *(also
    judgement) n.*
juice *n.*
jump *v.*
just *adv.*

K

keep *v.*
key *n.*
kick *v., n.*
kid *n., v.*
kill *v.*
kilogram *(also* kilo*) n.*
kilometer *n.*
kind *n., adj.*
kindness *n.*
king *n.*
kiss *v., n.*
kitchen *n.*
knee *n.*
knife *n.*
knock *v., n.*
knot *n.*
know *v.*
knowledge *n.*

L

lack *n.*
lady *n.*
lake *n.*
lamp *n.*
land *n., v.*
language *n.*
large *adj.*
last *adj., adv., n., v.*
late *adj., adv.*
later *adv.*

laugh *v.*
laundry *n.*
law *n.*
lawyer *n.*
lay *v.*
layer *n.*
lazy *adj.*
lead /lid/ *v.*
leader *n.*
leaf *n.*
lean *v.*
learn *v.*
least *adj., pron., adv.*
    at least
leather *n.*
leave *v.*
left *adj., adv., n.*
leg *n.*
legal *adj.*
legally *adv.*
lemon *n.*
lend *v.*
length *n.*
less *adj., pron., adv.*
lesson *n.*
let *v.*
letter *n.*
level *n.*
library *n.*
lid *n.*
lie *v., n.*
life *n.*
lift *v.*
light *n., adj., v.*
lightly *adv.*
like *prep., v., conj.*
likely *adj.*
limit *n., v.*
line *n.*
lip *n.*
liquid *n., adj.*
list *n., v.*
listen *v.*
liter *n.*
literature *n.*
little *adj., pron., adv.*
    a little
live /lɪv/ *v.*
living *adj.*
load *n., v.*
loan *n.*
local *adj.*
lock *v., n.*
lonely *adj.*
long *adj., adv.*
look *v., n.*
loose *adj.*
lose *v.*
loss *n.*

lost *adj.*
lot *pron., adv.*
  a lot (of)
  lots (of)
loud *adj.*
loudly *adv.*
love *n., v.*
low *adj., adv.*
luck *n.*
lucky *adj.*
lump *n.*
lunch *n.*

M

machine *n.*
magazine *n.*
magic *n., adj.*
mail *n., v.*
main *adj.*
mainly *adv.*
make *v.*
male *adj., n.*
man *n.*
manage *v.*
manager *n.*
many *adj., pron.*
map *n.*
mark *n., v.*
market *n.*
marriage *n.*
married *adj.*
marry *v.*
match *n., v.*
material *n.*
math *n.*
mathematics *n.*
matter *n., v.*
may *modal v.*
maybe *adv.*
me *pron.*
meal *n.*
mean *v.*
meaning *n.*
measure *v., n.*
measurement *n.*
meat *n.*
medical *adj.*
medicine *n.*
medium *adj.*
meet *v.*
meeting *n.*
melt *v.*
member *n.*
memory *n.*
mental *adj.*
mention *v.*
mess *n.*
message *n.*
messy *adj.*

metal *n.*
method *n.*
meter *n.*
middle *n., adj.*
midnight *n.*
might *modal v.*
mile *n.*
milk *n.*
mind *n., v.*
mine *pron.*
minute *n.*
mirror *n.*
Miss *n.*
miss *v.*
missing *adj.*
mistake *n.*
mix *v.*
mixture *n.*
model *n.*
modern *adj.*
mom *n.*
moment *n.*
money *n.*
month *n.*
mood *n.*
moon *n.*
moral *adj.*
morally *adv.*
more *adj., pron., adv.*
morning *n.*
most *adj., pron., adv.*
mostly *adv.*
mother *n.*
motorcycle *n.*
mountain *n.*
mouse *n.*
mouth *n.*
move *v., n.*
movement *n.*
movie *n.*
Mr. *abbr.*
Mrs. *abbr.*
Ms. *abbr.*
much *adj., pron., adv.*
mud *n.*
multiply *v.*
murder *n., v.*
muscle *n.*
museum *n.*
music *n.*
musical *adj.*
musician *n.*
must *modal v.*
my *adj.*
myself *pron.*
mysterious *adj.*

N

nail *n.*

name *n., v.*
narrow *adj.*
nation *n.*
national *adj.*
natural *adj.*
nature *n.*
navy *n.*
near *adj., adv., prep.*
nearby *adj., adv.*
nearly *adv.*
neat *adj.*
neatly *adv.*
necessary *adj.*
neck *n.*
need *v., n.*
needle *n.*
negative *adj.*
neighbor *n.*
neither *adj., pron., adv.*
nerve *n.*
nervous *adj.*
net *n.*
never *adv.*
new *adj.*
news *n.*
newspaper *n.*
next *adj., adv., n.*
nice *adj.*
night *n.*
no *exclamation, adj.*
nobody *pron.*
noise *n.*
noisy *adj.*
noisily *adv.*
none *pron.*
nonsense *n.*
no one *pron.*
nor *conj.*
normal *adj.*
normally *adv.*
north *n., adj., adv.*
northern *adj.*
nose *n.*
not *adv.*
note *n.*
nothing *pron.*
notice *v.*
novel *n.*
now *adv.*
nowhere *adv.*
nuclear *adj.*
number (*abbr.* No., no.) *n.*
nurse *n.*
nut *n.*

O

object *n.*
obtain *v.*
obvious *adj.*

occasion *n.*
occur *v.*
ocean *n.*
o'clock *adv.*
odd *adj.*
of *prep.*
off *adv., prep.*
offense *n.*
offer *v., n.*
office *n.*
officer *n.*
official *adj., n.*
officially *adv.*
often *adv.*
oh *exclamation*
oil *n.*
OK (*also* okay)
  exclamation, adj., adv.
old *adj.*
old-fashioned *adj.*
on *prep., adv.*
once *adv., conj.*
one *number, adj., pron.*
onion *n.*
only *adj., adv.*
onto *prep.*
open *adj., v.*
operate *v.*
operation *n.*
opinion *n.*
opportunity *n.*
opposite *adj., adv., n., prep.*
or *conj.*
orange *n., adj.*
order *n., v.*
ordinary *adj.*
organization *n.*
organize *v.*
organized *adj.*
original *adj., n.*
other *adj., pron.*
otherwise *adv.*
ought to *modal v.*
ounce *n.*
our *adj.*
ours *pron.*
ourselves *pron.*
out *adj., adv.*
out of *prep.*
outside *n., adj., prep., adv.*
oven *n.*
over *adv., prep.*
owe *v.*
own *adj., pron., v.*
owner *n.*

P

pack *v., n.*
package *n.*

page *n.*
pain *n.*
painful *adj.*
paint *n., v.*
painter *n.*
painting *n.*
pair *n.*
pale *adj.*
pan *n.*
pants *n.*
paper *n.*
parent *n.*
park *n., v.*
part *n.*
   take part (in)
particular *adj.*
particularly *adv.*
partly *adv.*
partner *n.*
party *n.*
pass *v.*
passage *n.*
passenger *n.*
passport *n.*
past *adj., n., prep., adv.*
path *n.*
patient *n., adj.*
pattern *n.*
pause *v.*
pay *v., n.*
payment *n.*
peace *n.*
peaceful *adj.*
pen *n.*
pencil *n.*
people *n.*
perfect *adj.*
perform *v.*
performance *n.*
perhaps *adv.*
period *n.*
permanent *adj.*
permission *n.*
person *n.*
personal *adj.*
personality *n.*
persuade *v.*
pet *n.*
phone *n.*
photo *n.*
photograph *n.*
phrase *n.*
physical *adj.*
physically *adv.*
piano *n.*
pick *v.*
   pick sth up
picture *n.*
piece *n.*

pig *n.*
pile *n.*
pilot *n.*
pin *n.*
pink *adj., n.*
pint *n.*
pipe *n.*
place *n., v.*
   take place
plain *adj.*
plan *n., v.*
plane *n.*
planet *n.*
plant *n., v.*
plastic *n.*
plate *n.*
play *v., n.*
player *n.*
pleasant *adj.*
please *exclamation, v.*
pleased *adj.*
pleasure *n.*
plenty *pron.*
pocket *n.*
poem *n.*
poetry *n.*
point *n., v.*
pointed *adj.*
poison *n., v.*
poisonous *adj.*
police *n.*
polite *adj.*
politely *adv.*
political *adj.*
politician *n.*
politics *n.*
pollution *n.*
pool *n.*
poor *adj.*
popular *adj.*
port *n.*
position *n.*
positive *adj.*
possibility *n.*
possible *adj.*
possibly *adv.*
post *n.*
pot *n.*
potato *n.*
pound *n.*
pour *v.*
powder *n.*
power *n.*
powerful *adj.*
practical *adj.*
practice *n., v.*
prayer *n.*
prefer *v.*
pregnant *adj.*

preparation *n.*
prepare *v.*
present *adj., n., v.*
president *n.*
press *n., v.*
pressure *n.*
pretend *v.*
pretty *adv., adj.*
prevent *v.*
previous *adj.*
price *n.*
priest *n.*
principal *n.*
print *v.*
priority *n.*
prison *n.*
prisoner *n.*
private *adj.*
prize *n.*
probable *adj.*
probably *adv.*
problem *n.*
process *n.*
produce *v.*
product *n.*
production *n.*
professional *adj.*
profit *n.*
program *n.*
progress *n.*
project *n.*
promise *v., n.*
pronunciation *n.*
proof *n.*
proper *adj.*
property *n.*
protect *v.*
protection *n.*
protest *n.*
proud *adj.*
prove *v.*
provide *v.*
public *adj., n.*
   publicly *adv.*
publish *v.*
pull *v.*
punish *v.*
punishment *n.*
pure *adj.*
purple *adj., n.*
purpose *n.*
   on purpose
push *v., n.*
put *v.*

Q
quality *n.*
quantity *n.*
quarter *n.*

queen *n.*
question *n., v.*
quick *adj.*
quickly *adv.*
quiet *adj.*
quietly *adv.*
quite *adv.*

R
race *n., v.*
radio *n.*
railroad *n.*
rain *n., v.*
raise *v.*
rare *adj.*
rarely *adv.*
rate *n.*
rather *adv.*
reach *v.*
reaction *n.*
read *v.*
ready *adj.*
real *adj.*
reality *n.*
realize *v.*
really *adv.*
reason *n.*
reasonable *adj.*
receive *v.*
recent *adj.*
recently *adv.*
recognize *v.*
recommend *v.*
record *n., v.*
recover *v.*
red *adj., n.*
reduce *v.*
refer to *v.*
refuse *v.*
region *n.*
regular *adj.*
regularly *adv.*
relation *n.*
relationship *n.*
relax *v.*
relaxed *adj.*
release *v.*
relevant *adj.*
relief *n.*
religion *n.*
religious *adj.*
rely *v.*
remain *v.*
remark *n.*
remember *v.*
remind *v.*
remove *v.*
rent *n., v.*
repair *v., n.*

repeat *v.*
replace *v.*
reply *n., v.*
report *v., n.*
reporter *n.*
represent *v.*
request *n., v.*
require *v.*
rescue *v.*
research *n., v.*
reservation *n.*
respect *n., v.*
responsibility *n.*
responsible *adj.*
rest *n., v.*
restaurant *n.*
result *n., v.*
return *v., n.*
rice *n.*
rich *adj.*
rid *v.*: get rid of
ride *v., n.*
right *adj., adv., n.*
ring *n., v.*
rise *n., v.*
risk *n., v.*
river *n.*
road *n.*
rob *v.*
rock *n.*
role *n.*
roll *n., v.*
romantic *adj.*
roof *n.*
room *n.*
root *n.*
rope *n.*
rough *adj.*
round *adj.*
route *n.*
row *n.*
royal *adj.*
rub *v.*
rubber *n.*
rude *adj.*
   rudely *adv.*
ruin *v.*
rule *n., v.*
run *v., n.*
rush *v.*

S
sad *adj.*
sadness *n.*
safe *adj.*
safely *adv.*
safety *n.*
sail *v.*
salad *n.*

sale *n.*
salt *n.*
same *adj., pron.*
sand *n.*
satisfaction *n.*
satisfied *adj.*
sauce *n.*
save *v.*
say *v.*
scale *n.*
scare *v.*
scared *adj.*
scary *adj.*
schedule *n.*
school *n.*
science *n.*
scientific *adj.*
scientist *n.*
scissors *n.*
score *n., v.*
scratch *v., n.*
screen *n.*
search *n., v.*
season *n.*
seat *n.*
second *adj., adv., n.*
secret *adj., n.*
secretary *n.*
secretly *adv.*
section *n.*
see *v.*
seed *n.*
seem *v.*
sell *v.*
send *v.*
senior *adj.*
sense *n.*
sensible *adj.*
sensitive *adj.*
sentence n.
separate *adj., v.*
separately *adv.*
series *n.*
serious *adj.*
serve *v.*
service *n.*
set *n., v.*
settle *v.*
several *adj., pron.*
sew *v.*
sex *n.*
sexual *adj.*
shade *n.*
shadow *n.*
shake *v.*
shame *n.*
shape *n., v.*
   shaped *adj.*
share *v., n.*

sharp *adj.*
she *pron.*
sheep *n.*
sheet *n.*
shelf *n.*
shell *n.*
shine *v.*
shiny *adj.*
ship *n.*
shirt *n.*
shock *n., v.*
shoe *n.*
shoot *v.*
shop *v.*
shopping *n.*
short *adj.*
shot *n.*
should *modal v.*
shoulder *n.*
shout *v., n.*
show *v., n.*
shower *n.*
shut *v.*
shy *adj.*
sick *adj.*
side *n.*
sight *n.*
sign *n., v.*
signal *n.*
silence *n.*
silly *adj.*
silver *n., adj.*
similar *adj.*
simple *adj.*
since *prep., conj., adv.*
sing *v.*
singer *n.*
single *adj.*
sink *v.*
sir *n.*
sister *n.*
sit *v.*
situation *n.*
size *n.*
skill *n.*
skin *n.*
skirt *n.*
sky *n.*
sleep *v., n.*
sleeve *n.*
slice *n.*
slide *v.*
slightly *adv.*
slip *v.*
slow *adj.*
slowly *adv.*
small *adj.*
smell *v., n.*
smile *v., n.*

smoke *n., v.*
smooth *adj.*
   smoothly *adv.*
snake *n.*
snow *n., v.*
so *adv., conj.*
soap *n.*
social *adj.*
society *n.*
sock *n.*
soft *adj.*
soil *n.*
soldier *n.*
solid *adj., n.*
solution *n.*
solve *v.*
some *adj., pron.*
somebody *pron.*
somehow *adv.*
someone *pron.*
something *pron.*
sometimes *adv.*
somewhere *adv.*
son *n.*
song *n.*
soon *adv.*
   as soon as
sore *adj.*
sorry *adj.*
sort *n., v.*
sound *n., v.*
soup *n.*
south *n., adj., adv.*
southern *adj.*
space *n.*
speak *v.*
speaker *n.*
special *adj.*
speech *n.*
speed *n.*
spell *v.*
spend *v.*
spice *n.*
spider *n.*
spirit *n.*
spoil *v.*
spoon *n.*
sport *n.*
spot *n.*
spread *v.*
spring *n.*
square *adj., n.*
stage *n.*
stair *n.*
stamp *n.*
stand *v., n.*
standard *n., adj.*
star *n.*
stare *v.*

start *v., n.*
state *n., v.*
statement *n.*
station *n.*
stay *v.*
steady *adj.*
steal *v.*
steam *n.*
step *n., v.*
stick *v., n.*
sticky *adj.*
still *adv., adj.*
stomach *n.*
stone *n.*
stop *v., n.*
store *n., v.*
storm *n.*
story *n.*
stove *n.*
straight *adv., adj.*
strange *adj.*
street *n.*
strength *n.*
stress *n.*
stretch *v.*
strict *adj.*
string *n.*
strong *adj.*
strongly *adv.*
structure *n.*
struggle *v., n.*
student *n.*
study *n., v.*
stuff *n.*
stupid *adj.*
style *n.*
subject *n.*
substance *n.*
succeed *v.*
success *n.*
successful *adj.*
successfully *adv.*
such *adj.*
  such as
suck *v.*
sudden *adj.*
suddenly *adv.*
suffer *v.*
sugar *n.*
suggest *v.*
suggestion *n.*
suit *n.*
suitable *adj.*
sum *n.*
summer *n.*
sun *n.*
supply *n.*
support *n., v.*
suppose *v.*

sure *adj., adv.*
surface *n.*
surprise *n., v.*
surprised *adj.*
surround *v.*
survive *v.*
swallow *v.*
swear *v.*
sweat *n., v.*
sweet *adj.*
swim *v.*
switch *n., v.*
symbol *n.*
system *n.*

T

table *n.*
tail *n.*
take *v.*
talk *v., n.*
tall *adj.*
tape *n.*
task *n.*
taste *n., v.*
tax *n.*
tea *n.*
teach *v.*
teacher *n.*
team *n.*
tear /tɛr/ *v.*
tear /tɪr/ *n.*
technical *adj.*
technology *n.*
telephone *n.*
television *n.*
tell *v.*
temperature *n.*
temporary *adj.*
tend *v.*
terrible *adj.*
test *n., v.*
text *n.*
than *prep., conj.*
thank *v.*
thanks *n.*
thank you *n.*
that *adj., pron., conj.*
the *definite article*
theater *n.*
their *adj.*
theirs *pron.*
them *pron.*
themselves *pron.*
then *adv.*
there *adv.*
therefore *adv.*
they *pron.*
thick *adj.*
thin *adj.*

thing *n.*
think *v.*
thirsty *adj.*
this *adj., pron.*
though *conj., adv.*
thought *n.*
thread *n.*
threat *n.*
threaten *v.*
throat *n.*
through *prep., adv.*
throw *v.*
thumb *n.*
ticket *n.*
tie *v., n.*
tight *adj., adv.*
time *n.*
tire *n.*
tired *adj.*
title *n.*
to *prep., infinitive marker*
today *adv., n.*
toe *n.*
together *adv.*
toilet *n.*
tomato *n.*
tomorrow *adv., n.*
tongue *n.*
tonight *adv., n.*
too *adv.*
tool *n.*
tooth *n.*
top *n., adj.*
topic *n.*
total *adj., n.*
totally *adv.*
touch *v., n.*
tour *n.*
tourist *n.*
toward *prep.*
towel *n.*
town *n.*
toy *n.*
track *n.*
tradition *n.*
traffic *n.*
train *n., v.*
training *n.*
translate *v.*
transparent *adj.*
transportation *n.*
trash *n.*
travel *v., n.*
treat v.
treatment *n.*
tree *n.*
trial *n.*
trick *n.*
trip *n., v.*

trouble *n.*
truck *n.*
true *adj.*
trust *n., v.*
truth *n.*
try *v.*
tube *n.*
tune *n.*
tunnel *n.*
turn *v., n.*
TV *n.*
twice *adv.*
twist *v.*
type *n., v.*
typical *adj.*

U

ugly *adj.*
unable *adj.*
uncle *n.*
uncomfortable *adj.*
unconscious *adj.*
under *prep., adv.*
underground *adj., adv.*
understand *v.*
underwater *adj., adv.*
underwear *n.*
unemployment *n.*
unexpected *adj.*
unexpectedly *adv.*
unfair *adj.*
unfortunately *adv.*
unfriendly *adj.*
unhappy *adj.*
uniform *n.*
union *n.*
unit *n.*
universe *n.*
university *n.*
unkind *adj.*
unknown *adj.*
unless *conj.*
unlikely *adj.*
unlucky *adj.*
unpleasant *adj.*
until *conj., prep.*
unusual *adj.*
up *adv., prep.*
upper *adj.*
upset *v., adj.*
upstairs *adv., adj.*
upward *adv.*
urgent *adj.*
us *pron.*
use *v., n.*
used *adj.*
used to *modal v.*
useful *adj.*
user *n.*

The Oxford 2000 List of Keywords

usual *adj.*
usually *adv.*

V

vacation *n.*
valley *n.*
valuable *adj.*
value *n.*
variety *n.*
various *adj.*
vary *v.*
vegetable *n.*
vehicle *n.*
very *adv.*
video *n.*
view *n.*
violence *n.*
violent *adj.*
virtually *adv.*
visit *v., n.*
visitor *n.*
voice *n.*
volume *n.*
vote *n., v.*

W

wait *v.*
wake (up) *v.*
walk *v., n.*
wall *n.*
want *v.*
war *n.*
warm *adj., v.*
warn *v.*
wash *v.*
waste *v., n., adj.*
watch *v., n.*
water *n.*
wave *n., v.*
way *n.*
we *pron.*
weak *adj.*
weakness *n.*
weapon *n.*
wear *v.*
weather *n.*
website *n.*
wedding *n.*
week *n.*
weekend *n.*
weigh *v.*
weight *n.*
welcome *v.*
well *adv., adj., exclamation*
    as well (as)
west *n., adj., adv.*
western *adj.*
wet *adj.*
what *pron., adj.*

whatever *adj., pron., adv.*
wheel *n.*
when *adv., conj.*
whenever *conj.*
where *adv., conj.*
wherever *conj.*
whether *conj.*
which *pron., adj.*
while *conj., n.*
white *adj., n.*
who *pron.*
whoever *pron.*
whole *adj., n.*
whose *adj., pron.*
why *adv.*
wide *adj.*
wife *n.*
wild *adj.*
will *modal v., n.*
win *v.*
wind /wɪnd/ *n.*
window *n.*
wine *n.*
wing *n.*
winner *n.*
winter *n.*
wire *n.*
wish *v., n.*
with *prep.*
within *prep.*
without *prep.*
woman *n.*
wonder *v.*
wonderful *adj.*
wood *n.*
wooden *adj.*
wool *n.*
word *n.*
work *v., n.*
worker *n.*
world *n.*
worried *adj.*
worry *v.*
worse *adj., adv.*
worst *adj., adv., n.*
worth *adj.*
would *modal v.*
wrap *v.*
wrist *n.*
write *v.*
writer *n.*
writing *n.*
wrong *adj., adv.*

Y

yard *n.*
year *n.*
yellow *adj., n.*
yes *exclamation*

yesterday *adv., n.*
yet *adv.*
you *pron.*
young *adj.*
your *adj.*
yours *pron.*
yourself *pron.*
youth *n.*